FIRST STEPS IN CAKE DECORATING

FIRST STEPS IN
CAKE DECORATING

JANICE MURFITT

NEW HOLLAND

First published in 1993 by
New Holland Publishers (UK) Ltd
London · Cape Town · Sydney · Auckland

Garfield House
86-88 Edgware Road
London W2 2EA
United Kingdom

80 McKenzie Street
Cape Town 8001
South Africa

Level 1, Unit 4, 14 Aquatic Drive
Frenchs Forest, NSW 2086
Australia

218 Lake Road
Northcote, Auckland
New Zealand

ISBN 1 85238 391 7 (hb)
ISBN 1 85238 548 0 (pb)

Editorial Director: Joanna Lorenz
Editor: Judith Simmons
Home Economist: Janice Murfitt
Designer: Bobbie Colgate-Stone
Photographer: Chris Turner
Illustrator: King & King Associates

Printed and bound in Singapore by Kyodo Printing Co (Pte) Ltd

Author's Acknowledgments
The author would like to thank Mavis Giles for her unfailing ability to type
illegible copy at a minute's notice, and for supplying equipment and
cake-icing and decorating props Jean Ainger at Cake Fayre.

CONTENTS

INTRODUCTION

THE FIRST STEPS in cake decorating are always the most important. Once these basic steps have been perfected, they will not only give you a good grounding for the subject, but the confidence and experience to master the more advanced techniques of this craft.

With clear techniques to follow, cake making, icing and decorating should be a pleasure and a joy to learn. Methods, equipment and materials are rapidly changing from day to day. New ready-made icings are being produced for easier modelling; modelling equipment and cutters are being continually updated, making it easier to reproduce beautiful flower decorations in sugar and flower paste; and food colourings appear in an ever growing range of colours and types.

This book has been designed using the most up-to-date methods of cake making, icing and decorating, taking you through all the basic techniques step by step, starting with equipment, planning cake designs and making templates for celebration cakes.

The basic cake is as important as the icing and decorating – each cake must always be worthy of decoration. The simple steps for shaping, cutting, filling and layering cakes are clearly described in the second section, giving a wide variety of cakes, gateaux, individual cakes and novelty shapes to choose from.

This leads on to the special occasion cakes, showing the steps for preparing a cake ready for decoration, including how to cover cakes with marzipan, sugar paste and royal icing for a professional finish. Methods for round, square and unusual-shaped cakes with various finishes are all detailed.

The choice of food colourings is quite complex these days and the next section gives clear advice on the types available and how to use them with a wide variety of different icings. Instant or last-minute decorations are an invaluable standby for everyday cakes or for when time is at a premium. By carefully selecting the right ingredients, the effects can be extremely attractive.

No book would be complete without a chocolate chapter. Who can resist the smooth, velvety finish of a cake covered with chocolate curls, leaves or chocolate dipped fruit? See how easy the techniques are by following the step-by-step photographs.

The remaining sections cover more advanced work using sugar paste for frills, cut-outs and extension pieces as well as marzipan modelling. The piping section covers in detail the many different ways cakes may be decorated with piped designs, including delicate line work, run-outs, embroidery, piped flowers and motifs. Flower paste is a wonderful icing medium for making all types of simple flowers, moulded flowers, cut-outs and wired flower sprays. With care, any type of fresh flower may be made by one of these methods to produce stunning and realistic results.

The recipes in the last section have been tried and tested to give excellent results every time, and a few tips have been highlighted which you may find useful when making or icing cakes.

I hope this book gives hours of pleasure and many ideas and designs for different cakes. And I am sure that by following the First Steps in Cake Decorating you will quickly perfect the techniques and achieve the attractive and professional results every cake decorator desires.

GETTING STARTED

With any craft, and cake icing and decorating is no exception, there are a number of basic principles which will help to ensure successful results every time. First, using good-quality equipment and materials is a must and here you will find sound advice for buying and hiring the basics. In addition, a beautiful cake rarely just materializes; for the best results, you will need to plan cake designs in detail right from the choice of cake base to the most subtle of decorative touches. This chapter will serve as a useful starting point to planning a cake to suit perfectly the person or occasion for which it is made.

CAKE-ICING EQUIPMENT

To obtain the very best results when icing cakes it is essential to have the correct specialist equipment. Although a vast selection of equipment is available from various types of outlets, it is best to purchase from specialist shops dealing in the craft of cake icing and decorating.

The professional equipment stocked by such shops is expensive, but will undoubtedly help you produce good results. The best equipment, carefully used and stored, will also last for a very long time and may never need to be replaced and will thus pay for itself several times over in its lifetime.

Although there are several companies selling specialist equipment by mail order, as a beginner it is best to go to the equipment shop to examine the items you require before actually buying them. Start off with the following: a turntable, a straight edge,

one plain and one patterned side scraper, an acrylic board and rolling pin, a set of crimpers, and a small selection of icing tubes. Such basic items will enable you to use royal icing or sugar paste and crimp or pipe a design.

As your cake-icing skills improve, purchase more equipment as and when it is needed, and you will quickly build up a good 'tool box'.

CARE OF EQUIPMENT

Cake-icing equipment must always be used, washed and stored with great care to avoid damage and to ensure that it lasts. Keep all the cake-icing equipment together in a spotlessly clean dry place away from any cold damp areas. Keep icing tubes in a box specially designed to keep them upright as this helps prevent the ends being damaged. (It also allows you to see at a glance the one you require.) Always clean them with a tube brush specially designed to clean the pointed ends without damaging them. Thor-

oughly dry all equipment – tubes, crimpers, cutters, tins (pans) and anything else made of metal – or they will rust and become discoloured and this, in turn, might well mark or stain future icing or sugar work.

Store acrylic or plastic boards flat in a dry place to prevent them warping or being scratched. Scratched acrylic or plastic surfaces harbour dirt and may impart impurities to the sugar work.

Wash and dry muslin (cheesecloth) and fabric piping bags thoroughly. Damp items will encourage the growth of moulds and discoloration.

Store straight edges and side scrapers carefully to prevent any damage to their surfaces; otherwise this will affect the smoothness of royal icing when pulled across the surface.

Have weighing scales regularly serviced or checked for accurate measurement of ingredients. Use either standard metric or imperial weights only. Do not mix the two as conversions are only approximate and even small differences could ruin a recipe.

SPECIAL EQUIPMENT FOR ICING

Before embarking on any form of cake icing or decorating, it is necessary to have a good selection of icing equipment to achieve good results.

Turntable: this is the most essential piece of equipment for easy movement of cakes while icing and decorating. Although expensive, a good turntable will last for ever and is obtainable from most kitchen shops or cake-icing specialists. Buy the best quality you can afford; check that the turntable is stable and make sure it revolves smoothly as this is essential when applying royal icing to the side of a round cake.

Straight edge: these are rigid and will not scratch or bend when being used on top of a cake to obtain flat, smooth royal icing. They are available in various lengths; as a general rule the 30 cm (12 in) straight edge is easier to handle on cakes up to 25 cm (10 in) in size. Those made from stainless steel are best.

Side scraper: these are made from plastic or stainless steel and used for smoothing icing on the sides of a cake. The plastic versions are more flexible and easier to use.

Patterned side scrapers: these come in a variety of designs and are ideal for finishing the sides of an iced cake with different patterns.

Muslin (cheesecloth): ideal for covering a bowl of royal icing to prevent a skin forming, and being white will not impart any colour to it. Keep the muslin clean and dry while in storage.

Brushes: fine artists' brushes, available in many different sizes from cake-icing specialists, have many uses for painting flowers and plaques with food colouring; they are also useful when making icing run-outs.

Flower nail: this can be homemade using a wine cork and a large nail; otherwise buy one from a kitchen shop or a cake-icing specialist. They are invaluable when piping flowers.

Small cutters: these are used for cutting out various shapes in sugar paste, marzipan, chocolate or fruit zest to use as decorations, and also come as numbers and letters. Tiny specialist cutters are available for making cut-out flowers from sugar paste and marzipan.

Tweezers: these are indispensable for delicate work; buy a pair with rounded ends.

Stamens: these can be bought in different colours and finishes from cake-decorating specialists and are used in the centre of moulded and cut-out sugar flowers.

Dowelling: different thicknesses of wooden dowelling are useful for drying leaves and petals over, to give them a more realistic curved shape.

Acrylic skewers: are used to support the tiers of a cake covered in sugar paste. They are hygienic as they are easily cleaned and can be cut to size before being covered with the cake pillars.

Florists' wire: available from cake-icing specialists, this comes in various gauges and colours for wiring sugar flowers on to stems and for making floral sprays.

Piping bags: these are made in a variety of materials, but the nylon ones are soft and flexible, making them suitable for cream, meringue and icing. Buy small, medium and large piping bags. Piping bags can be made easily from greaseproof paper and used with a variety of straight-sided tubes, or even without a tube.

Large tubes: buy a simple selection of small straight-sided star-shaped metal meringue tubes, varying in size but not too large. These will fit nylon piping bags and are ideal for piping cream, meringues and butter icing.

Fine tubes: straight-sided metal tubes are the best type to buy because they produce clean, sharp results and they fit into greaseproof-paper piping bags. They are available in a range of different designs and sizes.

Tube brush: essential for cleaning icing tubes without risk of bending or distorting the ends.

Icing syringe: usually available as a set including a selection of tubes, these are ideal for simple piping.

Crimpers: these come in a variety of different shapes and sizes from mini to maxi crimpers, offering many different patterns. They may come in a boxed selection, or can be purchased individually.

Acrylic rolling pin and board: ideal for rolling out small pieces of sugar paste or marzipan for decorations as the surfaces are non-stick. They are available in different sizes and although expensive, are easy to clean and practical to use.

Cake smoother: this is invaluable for smoothing sugar paste to obtain a flawless glossy surface.

Cake pillars: made from plastic these may be round, square or octagonal, usually with a hole through the centre so they can be slotted over the acrylic skewers which support a wedding cake covered with sugar paste; plaster cake pillars which have a clean, crisp finish are ideal for royal-iced wedding cakes.

Cake-Icing Equipment

1 Acrylic rolling pin
2 Acrylic board
3 Cake smoother
4 Florists' wires in various gauges and colours
5 Patterned and plain side scrapers in plastic and stainless steel
6 Tube brush
7 Fine straight-sided metal tubes in a variety of sizes and designs
8 Greaseproof-paper piping bags
9 Florists' tape
10 Stamens
11 Turntable
12 Garrette frill cutter
13 Fluted cutter
14 Cutting knife
15 Rounded-end tweezers
16 Crimpers
17 Small scissors
18 Scribing tool
19 Modelling tools
20 Acrylic skewers
21 Flower nail
22 Flower cutters
23 Artists' brushes
24 Stainless-steel straight edge
25 Small cutters
26 Large piping tubes
27 Nylon piping bag

INITIAL PLANNING

Before embarking on the making of a celebration cake, it is essential to think through the whole idea and plan every detail carefully. It is so easy to rush into making the cake with little thought of the final shape, size or finish.

There are many factors to be considered in the planning stages:

- The type of person the cake is for and their age.
- The cake mixture required for the cake.
- The shape and size of the cake.
- The occasion for which the cake is being made.
- The colour scheme and type of icing required.
- The design and the time available to complete the cake.
- Transportation of the cake and the distance of its destination.

All these factors must be carefully assessed and decisions made before you even buy the ingredients.

The type of person for whom you are making the cake is a fundamental influence – and obviously the age and gender are very important. The recipient may also have a particular interest, skill or hobby to which the finished cake can relate.

Design Inspiration
In the collection of items shown here each has a design, pattern or print which could be used when planning a cake design. Lace designs may be used to make piped lace pieces; pieces of embroidery or embroidery transfer designs can form the basis of a piped design. Designs on china can inspire border piping or broderie anglaise work. Fabrics, wallpapers and greetings cards offer bold prints which in turn may be adapted for run-outs, cut-outs or motifs for plaques or food colouring pen designs.

The type of cake mixture is also influenced by the recipient, perhaps a light sponge cake for a child or a rich fruit cake for an older person, giving it an especially personal theme.

The shape of the cake is all-important and there are so many shapes to choose from: hexagonal, round, square, oval, horseshoe, heart, petal, to name just a few. Special shaped tins may be hired from kitchen shops or cake specialists for a small charge or hire fee. Remember it is important to make sure the corresponding shaped cake boards are available, too.

The occasion for which the cake is being made dictates the type of cake you are making – whether it be a wedding, christening, anniversary or birthday cake. This goes hand in hand with the colour scheme. Discuss the base colour of the icing and the colours or shades of the decorations. If possible, try to acquire fabric samples or thread, flowers or ribbons, so that you have a guide to the colour scheme. Nothing is more disappointing than if the colours and shades of the cake do not match the décor, flowers or fabrics used elsewhere.

The design is always a personal aspect of cake decorating, and we all know our strong points and the skills with which we are happiest working. As the cake must be beautifully finished this should influence the design. It would not be sensible to attempt aspects of sugar craft in which you are not experienced. The time factor can also affect the design – if time is short, obviously a simple cake well finished is better than an intricate cake which is spoilt by being rushed at the last minute.

Bear in mind the destination of the finished cake before deciding on which decorations to use. Avoid fragile decorations like extension work for a cake which has to travel a long distance, as any breakage will spoil the design.

When all these factors have been considered, you can then confidently begin to devise the design for any cake in detail.

CAKE DESIGNING

A cake designed for a special event is often the centrepiece of the occasion. Prominently displayed, it will be viewed from all angles so it is essential to plan the design and decoration with this in mind.

It is often difficult to make a decision about the design as there are so many choices of decoration, cake shapes, colours, and techniques. However, once the shape and size of the cake have been decided, this gives you a base on which to plan your design. It can be easier if the design is left to you, but often suggestions are made about colour schemes, special requests for run-outs or sprays of flowers, so it is necessary to link these factors with the overall appearance of the cake.

The base colour of the cake has a strong impact on the finished design. Pastel shades or even white or champagne are the safest colours to choose for special occasion cakes, but try stronger colours for children's cakes and for novelty designs.

When it comes to the base covering there are three main choices – the clean, sharp classical lines of royal icing, the rounded, smooth finish of sugar paste or the softer effect of a butter-iced or frosted finish. These mediums dramatically change the appearance of the cakes and also the choices of the decoration. Run-outs look wonderful on a royal-iced cake, just as frills and flounces look perfect on a sugar paste cake and instant decorations, such as crushed nuts, crystallized (candied) or glacé fruits, and sugar-frosted flowers, complement simply iced (frosted) creations. If you need some inspiration for the design, it can be a good idea to look at fabric and wallpaper books for unusual floral or nursery designs, china or ceramic decoration, embroidery patterns – as all these designs can be interpreted in icing. Look at photographs of cakes in books and magazines, but avoid copying the whole of a design which appeals – mix and match ideas and techniques for your own personal designs.

Try simple designs to start with, using ribbons (see pages 69–71), embossing (see page 86) and crimping (see page 85); as your skills improve, try other designs.

Run-out motifs and letters (see pages 117–118), ribbon insertion (see page 94), collars and corner pieces (see page 118) or piped work (see pages 102–117) all require very accurate templates before embarking on the design. This requires a certain amount of geometry, carefully measuring and cutting; accuracy is the most important factor.

Cake Designing

The inspiration for this cake design was a furnishing fabric remnant. The fabric design has been simplified to make the pieces easier to cut out of sugar paste. The colours have been adapted, although these are a matter of choice, and the sugar paste coloured accordingly. The design was drawn on tracing paper to provide a template, then each piece of the design was cut out separately and applied to the dry sugar paste cake. To ensure the pieces fitted accurately, they were arranged together while still pliable and then pressed lightly into position.

MAKING AND USING TEMPLATES

Templates are often very useful for inscribing shapes and designs on the tops and sides of cakes.

Top templates: cut out a paper circle 2.5 cm (1 in) smaller than the top of the cake. Fold the circle in half and then twice more to make eight sections. Alternatively, fold the circle in half and then fold this semi-circle in three, to make six sections. You will always end up with a cone shape. To make a scalloped template, place a suitable round object at the base of the cone. Draw a pencil line round the shape and carefully cut it out. When the template is opened up, the edge will be scalloped. To adapt this design, place the round object half-way over the end of the cone shape and draw around the shape, rounding the curve inwards instead of outwards. This technique may be applied to a square template. To use the template, hold it gently on top of the cake and draw around it with a scribing tool. The outline can then be piped over with thread work and the shape could be filled in with trellis (see page 107) or cornelli work (see page 107), for example.

Top Templates

1 Cut out a circle of paper to the diameter of the cake, then trim off about 2.5 cm (1 in) all round.

2 Fold the circle to make 8 sections, then position a round object, such as a cup, so that the rim touches the base of the cone. Draw round the cup to form a curve.

3 Cut round the outline to form a scalloped template. Alternatively, draw an inverted curve on the base of the cone using either a small plate or a saucer.

4 To transfer the scalloped design to the top of the cake, draw round the template with a scribing tool.

1

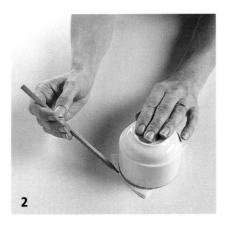

2

3

4

Side templates: making a template is a simple process. You need to cut a piece of greaseproof paper to exactly the height and the circumference of the cake. This strip of paper must fit absolutely accurately around the cake before making the template. If you are making frills to decorate cake sides (see pages 91–93), you will need a template to determine exactly where the frills will be applied. Fold the side template into as many sections as there are to be frills around the cake. Place a rounded object half-way over the base of the folded template and draw around it with a pencil to make the shape you require. Cut this out accurately, fix to the cake and scribe the scalloped drops to make the frill spacing or as a guide for piping dropped-loop thread work.

Side Templates

1 Make a paper template to the exact height and circumference of the cake. To form a scalloped side template for spacing frills or for a scalloped piping design, fold the strip into as many sections as you need.

2 Draw round a cup or other suitable round object to form an inverted curve, and cut carefully round the outline.

3 Fix the template to the cake and follow the scalloped outline with a scribing tool. The marked 'drops' can be used for positioning sugar paste frills or as a guide for piping work.

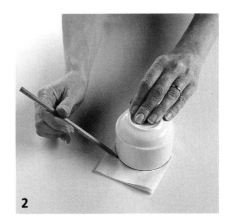

2

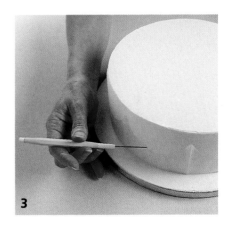

3

1

Other templates: as each cake varies slightly in size, run-out collar templates (see page 118) have to be designed each time to fit the cake you are decorating. First measure the top of the cake and draw it on a paper template, then add the collar design, allowing another 5 cm (2 in) all round the template to incorporate the design. These usually consist of scallops inwards and outwards, or hexagonal, round or square shapes.

For ribbon insertion (see page 94), the template must fit the top and sides of the cake. Accurately draw two lines the width of the ribbon and mark in the spaces where the ribbon is to be inserted. Use straight lines or curved lines, but ensure the measurements are correct, otherwise when the design is transferred to the cake, the ribbon pieces will look uneven.

Always keep templates once they are made, and write on them the size of cake for which each was used, so that they may be used again at a later date, or perhaps even adapted to fit a square cake instead of a round cake.

SHAPING, FILLING AND SIMPLE ICING

With a little imagination, everyday cakes can be totally transformed using a few simple techniques. For example, they can be cut and shaped to form simple geometric and curved shapes or more ambitious fun novelty designs. There are also many ways in which one or several cakes can be sliced and layered together with a variety of delicious fillings to produce very attractive effects once the cake is cut. Finally, there are many ideas for coating cakes with all types of icings and frostings to produce super smooth finishes or patterned effects.

SHAPING CAKES

Unusually shaped cakes, such as novelty cakes, fun cakes for adults or cakes for special occasions, require careful cutting and shaping. It is surprising the number of simple shapes that can be cut from a round or square cake, including novelty animals, such as mice, ladybirds, butterflies, all the numerals from 1 to 10, and clocks, cars, boats etc.

Cutting and shaping is always easier on a cake which has been made two or three days before, as this gives the cake time to settle.

Most types of cake may be cut into various shapes, although a simple quick-mix cake is the most reliable type to use for cutting regardless of its flavour or colour. Sometimes it is easier to bake the various shaped pieces in separate tins, bowls or moulds to obtain the necessary shapes, as whole uncut cakes are easier to work with.

When the cake is ready, work out exactly how it needs to be cut to form the required shape. Measure accurately as sometimes this is crucial to the end result. Measure and mark the cake, then cut the pieces carefully.

Always use a sharp straight-bladed knife to give a good clean cut. If there are any round, square or different shapes required, plain and fancy cutters are a good stand-by as they too give a good clean shape, making the assembly easier.

Brush all the pieces of cake with apricot glaze and leave them to dry before icing or covering with icing or frosting. The apricot glaze prevents the crumbs from the cut sides of the cake getting into the icing.

Assemble the pieces using apricot glaze, icing or frosting to form the cake into the shape required. Place the assembled cake on a cake board so that it does not have to be handled any more than is necessary.

At this stage the cake is ready to be covered with sugar paste, marzipan, butter icing or frosting, but do ensure the shape is maintained through the finishing process.

SIMPLE SHAPING

On occasion time does not allow tins (pans) to be hired to produce interesting shapes. However, simply cutting round or square cakes can create a wide variety of completely different shapes. Here are a few ideas.

- Cutting a square cake in half diagonally makes two triangles, and sliding them apart along the cut so that they only touch for about 10 cm (4 in) in the centre, produces a 'Z'-shape.
- Alternatively, placing the triangles back to back produces a diamond-shaped cake. ▶

● Cutting and arranging a round cake in the same way produces an 'S'-shape and an 'H'-shape respectively. Arrange the pieces of cake on a cake board and cover with marzipan and sugar paste or royal icing to decorate.

To Make a 'Z'-Shape

1 Cut a square cake in half diagonally to form two triangles. Slide them apart to produce a 'Z'-shape.

2 Brush the join with apricot glaze and assemble.

3 For a quick-and-easy finish, cover the cake with a flavoured butter icing or frosting and decorate as wished.

1

2

3

To Make an 'S'-Shape

1 Cut a round cake in half and slide the two halves apart to form an 'S'-shape. Brush the join with apricot glaze to assemble.

2 If covering the cake with sugar paste as here, brush the exposed surfaces of the cake with some more apricot glaze.

3 Smoothly coated with sugar paste (see pages 37–38), this makes a very pleasing shaped cake – ideal for someone whose name begins with 'S'.

1

2

3

Cutting Slab Cakes into Shapes

1 Bake a sponge cake in a 25 × 20 × 4 cm (10 × 8 × 1½ in) oblong tin (pan) so that the cake is about 2.5 cm (1 in) deep. Using various plain cutters with simple round and oval shapes, cut out shapes by pressing the cutter directly on the cake to cut the pieces out cleanly.

2 To cut the cake into triangles, squares etc, simply measure the sponge evenly. Cut it into strips and then cut into squares or other appropriate shapes. Cut some squares into triangles. When you have created the shapes of your choice brush all of them with apricot glaze to seal the edges. Cover with glacé icing and decorate the cakes with simple decorations.

1

2

Using Cutters to Make a Chequered Cake

1 Make two 18 cm (7 in) round sponge cakes in contrasting colours, say chocolate and plain. Using a plain pastry cutter with a diameter of 5 cm (2 in), carefully cut out a small round from the centre of each cake. Then use a similar cutter with a diameter of 10 cm (4 in) to cut out a further central ring from each cake.

2 Replace the cut-out pieces of cake, switching the middle ring of each cake for that of the contrasting colour, chocolate for plain and plain for chocolate. Brush each piece with apricot glaze before reassembling the cake.

3 Then sandwich the two cakes together, one on top of the other. Finish the cake with chocolate and plain butter icing, spreading the sides and coating with grated chocolate, and piping the top with contrasting butter-icing stars. When the cake is sliced, a perfect chequered pattern is revealed.

Chequered cake
Deceptively simple on the outside, a surprise awaits the person who cuts into this cake.

1

2

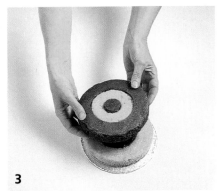

3

NUMERAL CAKES

Numeral cakes may be easily made from round, square or oblong sponge bases. If you like the numbers to have square edges instead of round, all the numbers may be cut from a 33 × 23 cm (13 × 9 in) oblong cake. Draw the number you require on a template and place it on the cake to cut out the shape or the pieces to make up the shape.

Number '3' Cake

1 To make a number '3', bake two 18 cm (7 in) round cakes or use the same size ring mould to bake two ring cakes. Using a 7.5 cm (3 in) plain cutter, remove a round from the centre of each. Cut one-third out of each of the rings of cake.

2 Position the two cut-out cakes as shown and cut away the excess, so the two pieces join together to make a '3'. When you are happy with your design brush the whole cake with apricot glaze and leave to set, and then cover with butter icing or frosting and decorate.

1

2

Tractor Cake

To cover and decorate the tractor, spread all the cake pieces with coloured butter icing and reassemble, pressing well together. Spread pairs of large biscuits, sandwiched together, with butter icing for the back wheels and repeat with smaller biscuits for the front wheels. Trim the cabin, the engine grille and the wheels with liquorice strips and use sweets for the wheel trims and headlights.

CUTTING NOVELTY CAKES

When designing and making novelty cakes, careful planning is vital. Work out the components of your selected design on paper and then decide what size and shape of cake or cakes will be needed. Trial and error is sometimes the only way to get the cake you envisage, but that is part of the fun.

Tractor Cake

1 Make a sponge cake in a 1 kg (2 lb) loaf tin (bread pan). Cut a 5 cm (2 in) piece off each end of the cake.

2 Trim one end piece to match the thickness of a mini chocolate-covered Swiss (jelly) roll. Brush all the pieces with apricot glaze.

3 To assemble the cake, position the mini Swiss roll crosswise on one side of the cake board with the trimmed-off piece at right angles to it to support the cabin. Arrange the cabin and engine housing on the supports to ensure all the pieces fit neatly.

1

2

3

LAYERING CAKES

Layered gâteaux or cakes are so appealing when they are cut into to reveal many different layers offering a variety of flavours and fillings. The selection can be endless – for example, layering chocolate sponge layers with vanilla, orange, lemon, lime or coffee or plain sponges with chocolate and coffee fillings to give sharp contrast in appearance, texture and flavour. To obtain a cake with perfect layers can sometimes be quite tricky but there are many ways of achieving the required end result.

A deep cake cooked in a single tin (pan) may be cut carefully into three layers or a cake mixture cooked in two sandwich tins may be divided into four layers. If the larger, more shallow Continental type of gâteau appeals, the thin cake layers (up to six) must be baked on baking sheets. Another interesting way of making a layered cake is to bake a Genoese sponge in a Swiss (jelly) roll tin and cut this across into three rectangular strips; when assembled it forms an oblong-shaped cake or gâteau.

To layer cakes successfully, it is essential to bake even-sized cakes with level tops, otherwise the layers will be uneven when the cake is assembled.

Always make sure the tins are even and are made of a good-quality metal.

Line the tins according to the cake mixture to be used as for some cakes they need to be fully lined while for others they need only to be lightly greased and dusted with flour. (See page 153 for more details.)

Make sure the mixture is spread level in the tin before baking. If a mixture needs to be divided into two or three tins, split the mixture evenly and then weigh the tins on scales to make sure.

If a cake mixture is being baked on baking sheets, first line them with baking parchment. Then draw circles to the diameter of each layer and ensure the mixture is spread to just inside these marked lines.

Do ensure the oven and the oven shelves are level so that the cakes do not bake unevenly.

Once the cakes are baked satisfactorily and cooled, cut them into layers if this is necessary. Place the cake on a thin cake board on a turntable at eye level. Using a long sharp knife, mark the number of layers required on the side of the cake. Cut into the side of the cake in a sawing movement as you slowly revolve the cake, keeping the cut level. Once you have cut all round the side of the cake, continue the sawing movement to separate the layers. Repeat to cut more layers if necessary.

If the layers are to be made by cutting across an oblong cake, measure accurately before cutting. Remember the old saying 'measure twice, cut once'.

Layering Two Cakes Together

1 Make a 20 cm (8 in) round chocolate cake and a 20 cm (8 in) round plain cake. Put one on a thin cake board and place this on a turntable at eye level. Mark a central line around the side of the cake. Using a sharp knife, cut just into the side of the cake while turning the turntable until one revolution has been completed. Then cut across the cake using a sawing movement to cut right through and produce 2 even layers. Repeat this procedure for the other cake.

2 Make a filling such as the *crème au beurre* used here and spread a base layer of plain cake evenly with some of this filling. Arrange a layer of chocolate cake on top. Repeat alternating layers until all are sandwiched in position. ▶

1

2

3 Always lift and position each layer carefully on top of the other, supporting them with the palms of both hands as shown here.

4 Check that the cake is level at each stage otherwise the cake will look uneven when finished. Chill at this stage to retain the shape. Finish the cake by coating it with the remaining *crème au beurre*.

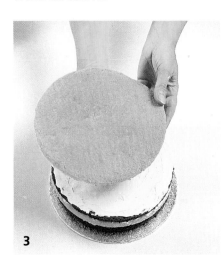

3

4

Layering an Oblong Cake

1 Make a sponge cake in a 33 × 23 cm (13 × 9 in) Swiss (jelly) roll tin (pan). Measure the cake carefully and cut it across into three equal strips. Roll out a piece of marzipan very thinly and cut it into three strips to match the cake layers.

2 Brush one layer of cake with warmed jam (jelly), then top with a layer of marzipan.

3 Spread the marzipan with cold chocolate icing. Then repeat the process with another layer of cake brushed with jam, and a layer of marzipan and chocolate icing.

4 Top with the last cake layer, jam and marzipan.

5 Roll out a thin length of marzipan to fit the sides of the cake, brush it with jam and fit smoothly in position. At this stage leave the cake to allow the marzipan to set. Finish by coating the cake in the remaining chocolate icing.

1

2

3

4

5

FILLING CAKES

Cake fillings come in different textures, consistencies, flavours and colours. As well as being an essential part of assembling a layered cake or gâteau, by sandwiching the layers back together to give the cake a good shape the filling also offers moisture and flavour.

Different fillings work better in some cakes than others; if a cake is light and delicate in texture, it needs to be filled with a light cream filling or frosting, while a more substantial cake will tolerate a richer type of filling. This factor is quite important when cutting a cake into portions as a heavy filling can often cause a cake to fall apart once cut.

There are many types of cake filling: whipped dairy cream with added coffee, chocolate or fruit zests; frosting flavoured with coffee, chocolate or citrus fruits; butter icing (which is the most popular), *crème au beurre* and chocolate fudge icing, not forgetting a variety of jams (jellies) which team well with all frostings and icings.

The consistency of a cake filling is important. When spread on the cut surface of a fresh cake, if a filling is too firm it will pull the crumbs from the cake, making an untidy layer; on the other hand, fillings which are too soft will cause the cake layers to slip and move around, and the filling to ooze out of the side of the cake.

To fill a cake, place the cake on a thin cake board. Use a palette knife dipped in hot water to spread the filling evenly over the cake. This prevents the filling from sticking to the knife and pulling up the cake crumbs. Dip the knife again in hot water and use it to obtain a smooth, level finish. Place the next cake layer in position, making sure it is level. Then repeat the procedure as necessary to fill the remaining cake. Always keep the cake on the cake board during filling to ensure the cake remains level and even at all times.

When dairy (whipping) cream is being used to fill a cake or gâteau, the most even way to fill the layers is to pipe the whipped cream evenly over the surface using a 5 mm (¼ in) plain piping tube. Place the next cake layer evenly in position and gently press to level. Repeat the procedure, filling and adding the remaining layers of cake as necessary.

Jam (jelly) for fillings should be heated gently to warm it and give it a softer consistency for spreading over the cake layers. If you are using jam and dairy cream for a filling, dilute the jam with a little water – warm jam will melt the cream.

The most important point to remember when layering and filling cakes is to work at eye level to ensure the cake is level. If the layers are even and the filling is spread evenly throughout the layers, and the cake is assembled ensuring all the layers are accurately put together, then the end result should be a well-shaped cake ready for coating.

Allow the filled cake to set in the refrigerator to ensure the cake is firm and retains a good shape before frosting or icing.

Filling a Layered Cake with Cream

1 Make a 20 cm (8 in) round cake in a deep cake tin (pan) or a *moule à manqué* mould. Place the cake on a cake board set on a turntable at eye level and mark the side with 3 even cuts. Then cut through the top layer first. You may find this easier if you have a thin cake board on top of the cake to hold it steady. Remove the top layer carefully before cutting the next layer.

2 Whip the cream until it is just standing in soft peaks and place it in a piping bag fitted with a 5 mm (¼ in) plain tube. Pipe the cream in a spiral coil on the base layer to cover it evenly.

3 Spread the underside of the next layer with jam. Place the next layer evenly in position. Repeat the process with the final layer. Chill the cake at this stage to set the cream before covering the cake in cream, nuts and piped cream.

Layers of soft sponge filled with tangy jam (jelly) and whipped dairy cream make a classic gâteau which is as pleasing to the eye as it is delicious.

COVERING CAKES WITH FROSTINGS AND ICINGS

One of the most satisfying parts of cake decorating is applying the finishing coat of icing or frosting before adding the final decorative touches to the cake. And a well-prepared cake comprised of even layers of cake and filling should be fairly easy to ice; it is always the preparation which makes the final process easy.

Frostings: these are quick icings usually beaten or whisked over hot water, melting or cooking the ingredients. Depending on the type of frosting being made, it may be a meringue type and quickly swirled, or a fluid frosting for a glossy smooth coating.

Icings: there are so many icings made with butter, egg whites, chocolate, and all types of flavourings, but they are all made with icing (confectioners') sugar and beaten together. The consistency of the icing may be anything from lightly whipped cream to stiff peak consistency which may be spread smoothly, swirled, piped, etc.

Again it is necessary to coat the cake with an icing which will complement the texture, flavour and filling of the cake. The same mixture used to fill the cake can often be used as the covering. It may first be necessary to dilute, thicken or warm the filling to obtain the desired finish to the cake.

Each frosting or icing has its own characteristic texture, flavour, colour and consistency. Some coverings are satin smooth and may be poured over the cake to give a smooth glossy finish. Other varieties may need spreading or swirling to give a textured appearance. Butter icing or creams may be smoothed flat, textured with a palette knife or piped to give a professional appearance. Whatever the choice of covering for the cake, have the base well prepared and cool rather than at room temperature to help ensure it keeps a good shape while being covered with icing.

USING FLUID ICINGS AND FROSTINGS

Covering cakes with frosting gives you a choice of a smooth surface or a textured finish. If the cake is to be smooth, keep it on a thin cake board the same size as the cake or slightly smaller, and place it on a cooling rack over a plate on a turntable.

Make the frosting, ensuring it is of the right consistency thick enough to coat the back of a spoon evenly. If it is too thick, place the bowl over hot water to melt the frosting (frostings are often already warm at this stage), or add a little water. On the other hand, if the frosting is too slack, allow it to cool so that it thickens.

Before actually frosting the cake, make sure everything is ready and there is a palette knife to hand. Pour the frosting all at once over the top of the cake and allow the frosting to fall freely over the sides. Do not be tempted to spread the frosting or it will mark, but gently tap or shake the cake to encourage the frosting to fall evenly from the top.

Once the frosting has stopped falling, run a palette knife around the base of the cake board to neaten the edge. Then allow the covering to dry. Carefully transfer the cake to a cake plate before adding the finishing touches.

To obtain a cake with a really sharp and defined shape, first spread some of the frosting over the cake to coat it evenly. Then, using a wetted palette knife, spread the icing as smoothly as possible to make a good shape. Leave this 'first coat' of frosting to set, then pour the remaining frosting over the cake as described above.

Glacé Icing Small Cakes

1 Glacé icing may be poured directly over small cakes, providing they have already been brushed with apricot glaze. However, a very thin layer of marzipan over the cakes ensures a really smooth finish. Small marzipan shapes may also be placed on top of some of the cakes for decoration.

2 Make plenty of glacé icing ensuring the consistency is thick enough to coat the back of a spoon with a transparent coat of icing which does not run off. Place the cakes, well spaced apart, on a cooling rack over a tray, plate or sheet of greaseproof paper. Using a cranked-handle palette knife to lift and support each cake, spoon the icing over in one movement.

3 Once all the cakes have been coated, leave them in position to dry. Carefully remove the icing from underneath the cakes before removing them from the cooling rack.

Tea-Time Fancies
These tiny, pretty cakes have been coated in pastel-coloured glacé icing. Simple threads of icing piped in contrasting shades complete the decoration.

Chocolate Icing with a Smooth Finish

1 Place the cake on a wire rack over a baking tray or on a plate set on the turntable. Make the chocolate icing, ensuring it is the right consistency to coat the back of a spoon. Pour the icing quickly over the cake to coat completely.

2 Shake the tray gently to encourage the icing to cover the cake evenly and smoothly; use a cranked-handle palette knife to smooth the surface, if necessary. When all the excess icing has stopped falling, carefully place the cake on a plate or a board. Allow the icing to set completely before decorating the top as wished.

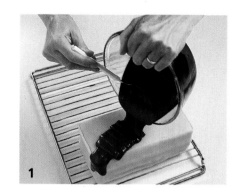

Feather Icing

1 Make the glacé icing to the correct consistency, slightly thicker rather than too slack or it will run off the cake. Tint one-quarter of the icing a deeper colour and place in a greaseproof-paper piping bag; fold down the top and have a pair of scissors ready. Pour the remaining icing over the top of the cake and, working fairly quickly, coax it to the edge of the cake with a paint brush so that the icing is completely level.

2 Snip the point off the piping bag and pipe parallel lines of icing across the top of the cake.

3 Draw a cocktail stick (toothpick) across the lines of icing in one direction and then in the opposite direction to create a feathered effect. Allow the icing to set.

Note: once glacé icing is set it has a tendency to crack when the cake is moved. It is therefore important to place the cake on a plate or board before icing it.

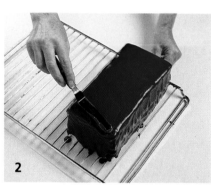

Covering a cake with icing of a thicker consistency is a different process as the icing needs to be spread evenly over the surface of the cake. First make sure the icing is well beaten, smooth and soft in texture (so that it does not pull up the surface crumbs of the cake). Keep the cake on a thin cake board and place this on the turntable. Place a spoonful of icing on top of the cake and use a small cranked-handle palette knife to spread this smoothly. Have to hand a jug of hot water into which to dip the knife as the icing is spread so that the icing does not stick to the palette knife and pull up the crumb surface.

Simply coat the cake evenly with the icing to obtain a smooth coating. Then, using the palette knife dipped into hot water, add some more icing and spread it smoothly to obtain a good, even surface.

A very attractive finish may be achieved by paddling the palette knife backwards and forwards to give a lined effect instead of a perfectly smooth coat. Another means of producing a pattern is to swirl the palette knife on the surface of the icing to produce a textured finish. Press small amounts of icing on the surface and pull the knife away sharply to produce a peaked finish.

Icing may also be piped over a cake to cover it. A basket-weave design is the most obvious choice as it covers the cake surface completely (see page 107). Lines of icing piped from top to bottom on the sides of the cake give an attractive finish, especially in conjunction with a smooth finish on top piped with a lattice-work design, for example (see page 107).

Once any cake has been covered, coating the sides with toasted nuts, crushed ratafias or meringues, crushed praline or grated chocolate adds flavour, texture and colour.

The cake is now ready for the finishing touches. Use any simple decorations, such as flowers, fruit, chocolate leaves or cut-out shapes.

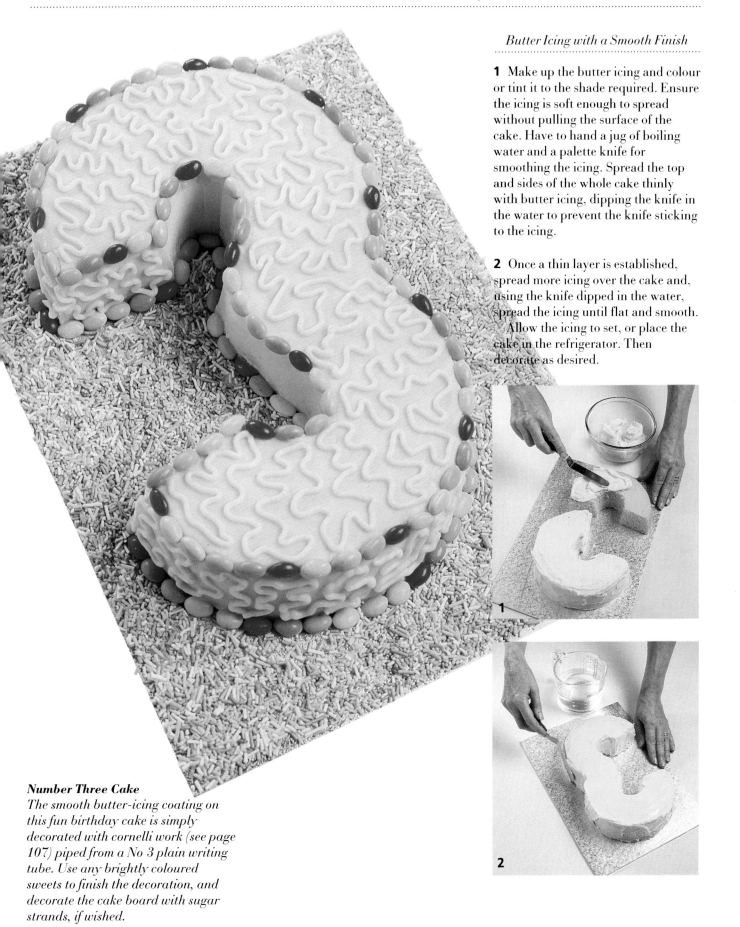

Butter Icing with a Smooth Finish

1 Make up the butter icing and colour or tint it to the shade required. Ensure the icing is soft enough to spread without pulling the surface of the cake. Have to hand a jug of boiling water and a palette knife for smoothing the icing. Spread the top and sides of the whole cake thinly with butter icing, dipping the knife in the water to prevent the knife sticking to the icing.

2 Once a thin layer is established, spread more icing over the cake and, using the knife dipped in the water, spread the icing until flat and smooth. Allow the icing to set, or place the cake in the refrigerator. Then decorate as desired.

Number Three Cake
The smooth butter-icing coating on this fun birthday cake is simply decorated with cornelli work (see page 107) piped from a No 3 plain writing tube. Use any brightly coloured sweets to finish the decoration, and decorate the cake board with sugar strands, if wished.

Crème au Beurre *with a Textured Finish*

1 Make a quantity of plain or chocolate *crème au beurre* and have to hand a jug of hot water and a palette knife. Spread the top and the sides evenly with the icing to cover the cake completely. Use the palette knife dipped in water to spread and smooth the icing so that a very flat surface is obtained.

2 Dip the clean palette knife in water and lightly run it backwards and forwards over the *crème au beurre* to create a lined effect.

Create the same lined pattern on the side of the cake, too, running the blade of the knife from the top of the cake to the base.

Flower Cream Gâteau
This gâteau looks fresh and tempting with a crème au beurre patterned finish and a piped reverse-scroll edging (see page 105). Ribbons and fresh flowers give a very quick and effective decoration, making this suitable to serve with coffee or tea.

Coating a Cake with Cream

1 Whip the dairy (whipping) cream until it peaks softly. Using a small palette knife, spread the sides of the cake evenly with cream.

2 Press toasted nuts on the side until the cream is evenly covered with nuts.

3 Spread the top of the cake with a layer of cream and use a palette knife to give a smooth finish to the surface. Place the remaining cream in a piping bag fitted with a small star tube and pipe a star border (see page 105) around the top edge.

Citrus Petal Gâteau
A light sponge is filled with freshly whipped dairy (whipping) cream and coated in lightly toasted flaked almonds. The top is piped with cream swirls and decorated with cut-out lime and orange zest petals and strips of orange and lime zest.

PERFECT CAKE COVERINGS

Special occasion cakes need very special coverings to provide a perfect finish and base for the piped, moulded and modelled decorations you eventually select to complete the cake. Two of the most popular coverings are sugar paste and royal icing and there are specific techniques for applying these to a cake base, whether it is round, square or a more unusual shape. For a really smooth finish it is always advisable to marzipan the cake prior to icing. Follow these techniques and tips for applying marzipan, sugar paste and royal icing and, with a little practice, your special occasion cakes will have that unmistakable professional touch.

MARZIPAN

Marzipan is a pliable paste made from ground almonds and a mixture of caster (superfine) and icing (confectioners') sugars. The exact consistency, texture and colour vary according to how the paste is made. It is used for modelling, decorating, for covering cakes to preserve them by keeping the moisture in, and to give a smooth, flat surface before applying royal icing or sugar paste.

Homemade marzipan: usually has a better flavour, being made with a higher proportion of ground almonds to sugar (see page 147). It may also be made in more easily manageable quantities. Care must be taken not to over-knead or over-handle the marzipan when making it. Over-kneading encourages the oils to flow from the ground almonds, giving an oily covering to a cake which will eventually seep through the icing, causing unsightly staining.

Ready-made marzipan: is now readily available in both white and yellow forms. Use the white marzipan for all types of cake as it is the most popular and reliable type to use, especially when cakes are being iced in pastel shades or white. The yellow marzipan has added food colouring and may be used for covering rich fruit cakes, but the yellow colour may show through if the icing is thinly applied or cause yellow staining on the surface. This yellow marzipan also does not take other food colourings as well as white marzipan when used for modelling work and decorations.

When covering a cake or modelling decorations, always use fresh pliable marzipan to obtain the very best results. To avoid waste, knead the trimmings together and seal them well in a plastic bag for further use. Be sure to allow the marzipanned cake to dry thoroughly before applying the icing. This is best done by storing the cake in a cardboard cake box in a warm dry room. Properly set marzipan ensures a good cake shape during icing and prevents any moisture seeping through from the cake and staining the surface. Ideally, allow up to 24 hours for the marzipan to set before applying any form of icing, and 48 hours before applying royal icing.

HOW TO MARZIPAN A CAKE FOR SUGAR PASTE

When applying marzipan to a cake which is to be covered with sugar paste, it is necessary to smooth the marzipan to the contours and shape of the cake to give a smoothly rounded finish. In this way, the final covering of sugar paste will not be marred by unsightly lumps and bumps.

This is very quick and easy to do as long as the marzipan is eased carefully over the sides, corners or edges of the cake, taking care not to stretch or tear the marzipan at any point. Make sure there are no air bubbles trapped underneath the marzipan on top of the cake before easing the marzipan down the sides.

Round or oval cakes are the most simple shapes to cover as they have the top and only one side to cover smoothly. Square, hexagonal, petal- or other shaped cakes are slightly more difficult to cover with marzipan because of the unusual sides or corners. To prevent the marzipan from stretching or tearing carefully cup your hands around the base of the corners and gently ease the marzipan up towards the top of the cake. But whatever the shape and size of the cake, the basic method is the same.

Method for Round Cakes

1 Unwrap the cake and remove any lining paper. Place the cake on an appropriate cake board and roll the top of the cake carefully with a rolling pin to give a flat surface. Brush the top and sides of the cake with apricot glaze, and dust the surface lightly with sieved icing (confectioners') sugar.

2 Knead the marzipan into a smooth ball. Roll out to a thickness of 5 mm (¼ in) in a shape matching that of the cake, and large enough to cover the top and sides with about 5–7.5 cm (2–3 in) extra all around. Make sure the marzipan is not sticking to the work surface, then roll it loosely around the rolling pin.

3 Place the supported marzipan over the cake and carefully unroll it from the rolling pin so that the marzipan falls evenly over the cake. Working from the centre of the cake, carefully smooth the marzipan over the top and down the sides, allowing the excess marzipan to spread out on the cake board.

4 Using a sharp knife and cutting down on to the board, trim the excess marzipan from the base of the cake.

5 Using clean dry hands or a cake smoother, gently rub the top of the cake with a circular movement to give a smooth glossy finish to the marzipan.

6 Leave in a warm dry place for at least 2 hours, or preferably up to 24 hours, before covering over with sugar paste.

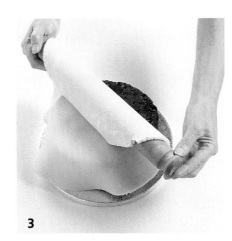

3

4

1

5

2

6

Tips for Cakes with Corners

1 Gently rub the sides of square and rectangular cakes, as well as the top, with your hands or a cake smoother.

2 For cakes with corners, carefully cup your hands around the base of the corners and gently ease the marzipan up towards the top to prevent stretching or tearing.

3 When trimming cakes with a complicated outline, take special care. Hold the knife upright and slowly follow the contours of the cake.

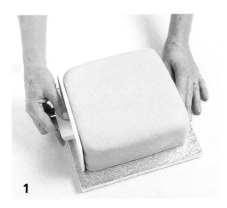

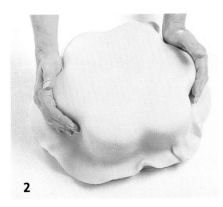

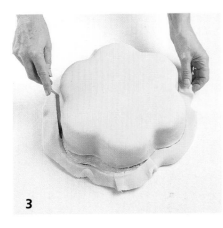

HOW TO MARZIPAN A CAKE FOR ROYAL ICING

Marzipanning a cake ready for royal icing is a very exacting process as the underlying shape of the cake is the key to the flat finish of the icing.

When covered with marzipan, the cake should look clean, sharp and smooth. This result is obtained by first marzipanning the top of the cake and then placing the cake on a cake board before applying the marzipan to the sides. The side of round cakes may be covered with one long strip of marzipan measured to the exact height and length of the side of the cake. Square cakes need four single pieces, one applied to each side of the cake and cut accurately for shape to ensure good square corners.

All the seams and joins should be smoothed together with a palette knife and the cake left to dry in a warm dry place for at least 48 hours. Dried and set marzipan will ensure a good shape before applying the royal icing.

Method for Round Cakes

1 Unwrap the cake and remove any lining paper. Place the cake on an appropriate cake board and roll the top of the cake carefully with a rolling pin to give a flat surface. Brush the top of the cake with apricot glaze. Lightly dust the surface with icing (confectioners') sugar.

Knead two-thirds of the marzipan into a round. Roll this out to a thickness of 5 mm (¼ in) to fit the top of the cake, allowing a little extra all round.

2 Make sure the marzipan is not sticking to the work surface. Then invert the cake and place it in the centre of the marzipan round. Trim off the excess marzipan to within 1 cm (½ in) of the cake. Then, using a small flexible palette knife, push the marzipan level to the side of the cake, until the marzipan forms a neat edge all round the cake.

Turn the cake over again so that the marzipan is on top and place in the centre of the cake board. Brush the sides with apricot glaze.

3 Knead the marzipan trimmings together, taking care not to include any crumbs from the cake. Measure and cut a piece of string to match the circumference of the cake. Measure and cut another piece of string the depth of the side of the cake from the board to the top.

Roll out the remaining marzipan to a thickness of 5 mm (¼ in) and cut out one side piece to match the length and width of the pieces of string. Knead the trimmings together. ▶

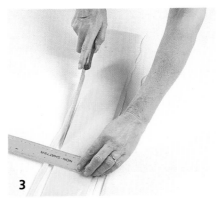

4 Carefully fit the marzipan strip on the side of the cake and smooth the join with a palette knife.

5 Leave in a warm, dry place for at least 48 hours before icing.

4

5

Method for Square Cakes

1 Unwrap the cake, place on an appropriate cake board and roll the top of the cake to flatten the surface. Brush the top with apricot glaze. Lightly dust the work surface with icing (confectioners') sugar.

2 Knead two-thirds of the marzipan into a square shape. Roll this out to a thickness of 5 mm (¼ in) to fit the top of the cake, allowing a little extra all round. Invert the cake on the marzipan and trim the excess to within 1 cm (½ in) of the cake sides. Push the marzipan against the cake sides with a palette knife to form a neat edge.

3 Measure the length and depth of one side of the cake. Brush the sides of the cake with apricot glaze and roll out the remaining marzipan. Measure and cut the four side pieces.

4 Carefully fit the pieces to the cake sides and smooth all the joins with a palette knife.

5 Leave the marzipanned cake in a warm, dry place for at least 48 hours before icing.

1

2

3

4

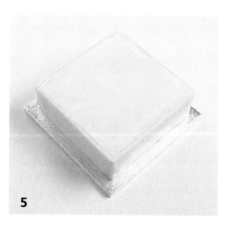

5

Golden Rose Cake
Ideal for a Golden Wedding cake, the royal icing with its crisp, classic lines is the perfect covering for an elegant celebration cake. The marzipan base and icing must be applied with great care to ensure an even finish. Decorated with a simple reverse-scroll border, the cake is trimmed with yellow ribbons and shaded yellow flower paste roses, flowers and sprays (see pages 122–135).

Petal Cake

Sugar paste is ideal for covering unusual shaped cakes; it is easy to apply and gives a wonderfully smooth and professional finish. This pretty petal-shaped cake would be perfect for a birthday, christening, anniversary or special occasion cake. This base comprises a 25 cm (10 in) rich fruit cake covered with marzipan and pale-pink sugar paste, simply piped with a shell border using a small star tube and white royal icing and decorated with deep-pink silk flowers and ribbons.

SUGAR PASTE

Sugar paste has become increasingly popular during the last few years. Originally from Australia, it is now widely used in many countries because of its versatility and ease of use. Celebration cakes are now often seen as softly rounded, smooth cakes instead of having the sharp crisp classical look of the traditional royal-iced cake.

There are many advantages when using this type of icing, the most obvious being that it is quick, easy and instant to use. Being soft and pliable, the icing may be rolled out to any shape and used to cover freshly marzipanned cakes to produce an instant result. The same straightforward method applies to cakes of every shape and size. Even the least-experienced cake decorator can achieve a smooth, glossy professional finish requiring the minimum amount of decoration to finish the cake. Trimmings need not go to waste; they may be coloured and used to make decorations such as frills, flowers and cut-out designs.

Although sugar paste is easy to make (see page 147), there are certainly times when the ready-made variety is better or more convenient to use. There are several types of sugar paste on the market, all basically the same recipe but packaged under many different names. Textures may vary and some are certainly better to handle than others. Before purchasing large amounts of any one brand it is a good idea first to try a small quantity to see if it is suitable for the cake you are icing.

Sugar paste may be purchased in 225 g (8 oz) packs from many supermarkets and shops, or in boxes of up to 5 kg (11 lb) from cake-icing specialists. When you have found a brand that you like, it is advisable to buy a large quantity because you will then be sure that all the sugar paste comes from the same batch and this will help to produce a smooth even finish.

Sugar paste will keep for several months as long as it is stored in an airtight container from which air is completely excluded.

Sugar paste is available in white, champagne, pastel and primary colours and many more – even black! If you need a large quantity for a wedding cake, to ensure the colour is even throughout carefully consider the amount of each colour you will require. Kneading food colouring into large quantities of sugar paste is hard work and time-consuming. It is also sometimes quite difficult to obtain an evenly blended colour without incorporating some air bubbles into the sugar paste.

If tinting sugar paste at home, knead the food colouring into a small piece of the sugar paste until it is darker than the colour required. Then knead the coloured piece into the remaining white sugar paste until the colour is even, the sugar paste is smooth and the correct shade has been obtained.

Sugar paste may be used to cover all types of cakes and for making decorations such as sugar flowers, leaves, cut-out sugar pieces or for modelling animals or figures (see pages 84–101).

Covering Cakes with Sugar Paste

1 Place the marzipanned cake on a matching shaped cake board and set on a turntable, if using. Brush the surface evenly with a little sherry or cooled boiled water

2 Dust a work surface with sieved icing (confectioners') sugar to prevent the sugar paste from sticking. Using more sieved icing sugar if necessary, roll out the sugar paste to a thickness of 5 mm (¼ in) and in a shape to match that of the cake with an overlap generous enough to cover the sides of the cake. Make sure the sugar paste is not sticking to the work surface.

Brush any excess icing sugar off the sugar paste and lift it, supported by a rolling pin. Unroll the sugar paste over the cake to cover evenly.

3 With hands lightly dusted with cornflour (cornstarch) smooth the sugar paste over the top and then down the sides of the cake so that the excess sugar paste is at the base, taking care to exclude any air bubbles between the surfaces. If the cake is square, allow the excess sugar paste to fall over the corners. Then, with cupped hands, smooth the sugar paste from the base of the corners up to the top. This will prevent the sugar paste tearing or stretching. Smooth the remaining sugar paste with a cake smoother. ▶

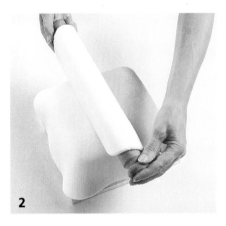

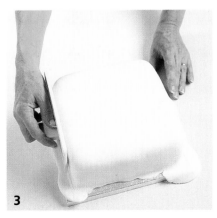

4 Using a small knife, trim off excess icing at the base of the cake. With hands lightly dusted with cornflour, gently rub the surface of the icing in a circular movement to give the icing a smooth and glossy finish.

5 Place the cake in a cake box and leave in a warm dry place to allow the sugar paste to dry. Knead the trimmings together and seal them in a polythene bag. They may then be used to cover the cake board or for decorations.

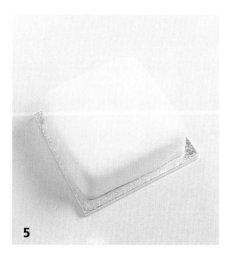

CAKE BOARDS

There are several ways in which a cake board may be covered with sugar paste to enhance the appearance of the finished cake.

The whole cake board may be covered with matching sugar paste with a smooth clean finish, and the cake then placed in the centre of the board. Alternatively, allow enough sugar paste to cover the cake and the board completely, trimming off the excess icing around the edge of the board.

Sugar frills (see pages 91–93) joined up and around the base of the cake to cover the board can give a very elegant look to a plain sugar-pasted cake. Trimming with ribbon at the join along the base of the cake gives a wonderful finishing touch.

Covering Cake Boards with Sugar Paste

1 Tint the sugar paste to the required colour to match the cake. Brush the cake board with a little apricot glaze.

2 Lightly dust a work surface with icing (confectioners') sugar. Roll out the sugar paste to a thickness of 5 mm (¼ in) and in a shape to match the cake board. Ensure the sugar paste is not sticking to the work surface and lift it over the cake board. Smooth the surface with hands lightly dusted with cornflour (cornstarch) or with a cake smoother.

3 Using a small palette knife, trim off the excess icing, keeping the blade level with the edge of the board and taking care to keep the edge of the icing straight.

4 Leave the iced board in a warm place overnight to dry, then place the iced cake carefully in position on it.

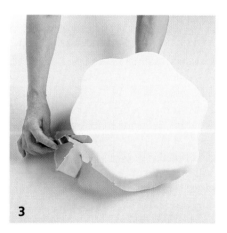

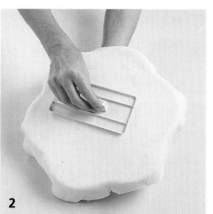

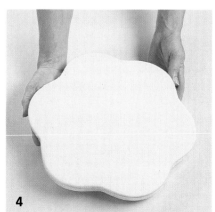

Covering a Cake and Cake Board Together

1 Follow the instructions for covering any shaped cake with sugar paste, but roll out the sugar paste so that it is large enough to cover the top of the cake, the sides and the cake board.

2 Carefully lift the sugar paste over the top of the cake, supported by a rolling pin. Unroll the sugar paste over the cake to cover it evenly.

3 With hands lightly dusted with cornflour (cornstarch), smooth the sugar paste over the top and down the side of the cake and over the surface of the cake board, taking care to exclude any air bubbles between the surfaces.

4 Using a palette knife, trim off the excess icing around the edge of the cake board, keeping the blade level with the edge of the board and taking care to keep the edge of the icing straight. Leave the iced cake and board to dry in a box in a warm, dry place overnight before adding your chosen decorations.

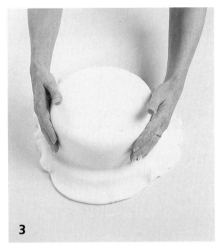
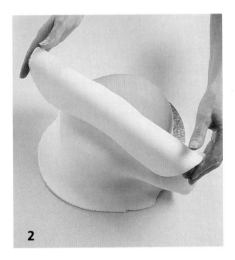
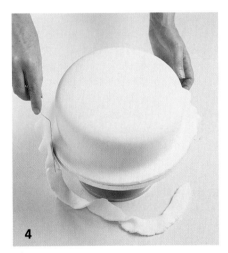

Harvest Cake
A 20 cm (8 in) marzipanned Madeira cake is covered with sugar paste applied to the cake and cake board together. The edge is simply crimped (see page 85), the cake board and cake are trimmed with yellow ribbon and an arrangement of marzipan fruit (see page 97) gives the cake its theme.

ROYAL ICING

A royal-iced cake is often preferred to a cake covered with sugar paste simply because of the crisp texture and taste of the icing. Although this method of icing is far more time-consuming and takes patience and practice, the end result is the instantly recognizable sparkling finish and classical lines of a more traditional type of celebration cake.

To produce a beautifully royal-iced cake, it is essential to have a well-prepared level cake which has been carefully marzipanned. The lines must be kept sharp, keeping the cake a good shape. The royal icing must be light and glossy in texture and of the correct consistency. With patience, practice and the right tools, a good result may then be achieved.

When making royal icing, everything must be spotless. All mixing bowls, sieves and utensils must be clean and dry, and the working area as dust-free as possible. Wear a white overall as little bits of clothing lint can get into the icing and will come to the surface on a flat coat of icing, or even cause the piping tubes to block.

Fresh egg whites or egg albumen may be used to make the icing, both producing good results. A little lemon juice helps to strengthen the albumen in fresh egg whites, but care must be taken not to add too much as this will make the icing short, causing it to break during piping, as well as making it difficult to obtain a smooth flat finish. Do not add glycerine to egg albumen as it will not then set as hard as fresh egg-white icing.

The icing (confectioners') sugar must be added gradually and the icing mixed well rather than beaten with each addition of sugar, until the required consistency has been reached and the icing is light and glossy in texture. A food mixer may be used (especially if large quantities of royal icing are required) at the lowest speed, until the icing is light, glossy and of the correct consistency. Take care not to over-mix or aerate the icing. Always allow mixer-made royal icing to stand for 24 hours before use, then stir it well to remove any air bubbles.

Royal icing made by adding too much icing sugar too quickly will form a dull heavy icing which is grainy in appearance. It will also be difficult to work with and produce inferior results. When set, it will be chalky and dull in appearance instead of having a sparkle. The icing will also be difficult to pipe, soon becoming short and breaking off.

The icing must be covered at all times to exclude air and to prevent the surface from drying and becoming lumpy. Use dampened clingfilm (plastic wrap) to seal the surface, or place the icing in an airtight container (as long as it is filled to the top with icing to exclude any air). Covering the icing with a damp cloth is satisfactory for short periods, but if it is left overnight the icing will absorb all the moisture from the cloth, diluting it.

Always check the icing regularly during use to make sure the consistency and texture are correct.

If the icing is too stiff, add egg white or reconstituted egg albumen to make it softer. If the icing is too soft, gradually stir in more sieved icing sugar until the required consistency has been reached.

Work from a small quantity of icing in a separate bowl from the main batch of royal icing, covering it with damp muslin (cheesecloth) during use. Keep the icing well scraped down into the bowl. If the icing does become dry around the top edges of the bowl, causing hard bits, it will not then affect the whole batch of royal icing.

ROYAL-ICING CONSISTENCIES

Consistency of royal icing is a very important factor as this may affect the result of the icing work – whether it is for flat, peaked or piped icing. The consistency required of royal icing varies for different uses: a stiff icing which will hold its shape is best for piping (see pages 104–117); a slightly softer icing which will spread smoothly when a straight edge is pulled across the top is better for flat icing and also for peaked icing (see page 45); an even slacker icing consistency is required for filling in run-outs (see pages 117–121).

Piping consistency: stir the icing well with a wooden spoon. When the spoon is drawn out of the icing, it should form a fine, sharp point. This consistency, termed· 'sharp peak', will flow easily for piping but retain the definite shape produced by the icing tube used.

Flat or peaked icing consistency: stir the icing well with a wooden spoon and when the spoon is drawn out of the icing it should form a fine point which just curves over at the top. This consistency, termed 'soft peak', spreads smoothly and evenly and creates a flat finish when a straight edge is pulled across the top. However, the same consistency of icing can be pulled up into soft peaks with a palette knife to produce peaked icing.

Run-outs: soft-peak consistency icing is used to pipe the outlines which retain the shape of the run-out. Then icing of a thick cream consistency is used to fill in the shapes. This consistency flows to fill in the run-outs, but holds a rounded shape within the piped lines. Always remember to make the icing for run-outs with double-strength egg albumen (dried egg whites), or use egg whites without glycerine so that the icing dries hard and the run-outs are easily removed without breakages.

Method for Square Cakes

1 Make a quantity of royal icing to soft-peak consistency and cover it with clean, damp muslin (cheesecloth). Place the marzipanned cake on the cake board.

2 Using a small palette knife, spread a small amount of icing back and forth across the top of the cake to eliminate any air bubbles. Then spread the icing as smoothly as possible over the top of the cake to cover the surface evenly.

3 With a small palette knife, remove the excess icing from the top edges of the cake to neaten them. Take the cake off the turntable, if using, and place it on a rigid surface.

4 With the cake directly in front of you, hold a straight edge comfortably by its top edge and place it at the far side of the cake. Steadily pull the straight edge evenly across the top of the cake in one continuous movement to smooth the icing. If the icing is not smooth enough, repeat the movement once again until it is smooth, or respread the top of the cake with a little more icing, neaten the edge once more and start again. Don't worry about this first layer being absolutely perfect; it just needs to cover the cake thinly.

5 With a clean palette knife, trim away the excess icing from the top edges of the cake to neaten. Then leave the icing to dry for about two hours or overnight in a warm dry place. Store it in a cardboard cake box to prevent the surface from being damaged or marked.

6 Replace the cake on the turntable, if using. Use a small palette knife to smoothly spread one side of the cake with icing to cover evenly.

7 Remove the excess icing from the dry icing on the top edge of the cake and at each corner.

8 Place the cake on a rigid surface and position a side scraper at the far corner of the cake so that it just rests on the cake board. Pull the side scraper across the freshly iced side of the cake in one movement to smooth the icing. If the surface is not satisfactory, repeat the process once again. Alternatively, re-spread the side of the cake with more icing, neaten the top edge and the corners and repeat again. ▶

1

2

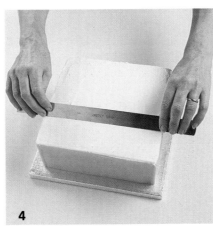

3

4

5

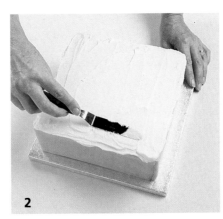

6

7

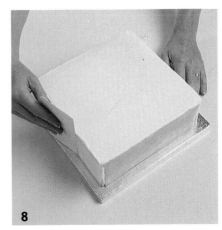

8

9 Trim away the excess icing from the top edge, the corners of the cake, and the cake board to neaten. Ice the opposite side of the cake in the same way. Neaten the edges and the cake board and leave to dry for at least two hours.

10 Ice the remaining sides of the cake in the same way. Leave the cake to dry overnight in the cardboard box before continuing the process.

Ice the cake with another two or three thin coats of icing in the same way, until the icing is smooth and flat. To obtain a really smooth final coat of icing, use a slightly softer consistency of icing, and this will skim the surface to leave it smooth and sparkling.

9

10

Method for Round Cakes

1 Royal icing a round cake is basically the same technique as that for a square cake, but easier and quicker as there are only two surfaces to ice. Follow steps 1 to 5 for royal icing the top of a square cake.

2 Using a small palette knife, spread the side evenly with the icing.

3 Neaten the top edge with a palette knife.

4 Replace the cake on the turntable. With one hand, hold the side scraper firmly against the side of the cake around the back, so that it just rests on the cake board. Hold the cake board and turntable with the other hand. Turn the cake and turntable continuously in the same direction for one whole revolution while holding the side scraper against the icing and pulling it towards you in the opposite direction to smooth the icing. Gently draw the side scraper off the cake. This will leave a slight mark.

5 Neaten the top edge and repeat the process again. Neaten the top edge and the cake board, and place the cake in a cardboard cake box to dry.

Leave the cake to dry before repeating the same procedure to cover the cake with another two or three thin layers of icing. Use a slightly softer consistency of icing for the final layer which will skim the surface to leave it smooth and sparkling.

1

2

3

4

5

Flower Design Cake

A pretty birthday cake for a daughter, mother, grandmother or any other female relative, this 20 cm (8 in) light fruit cake is covered with marzipan and smooth royal icing. The base and top edge are piped with a shell edging and the board and cake are trimmed with mauve ribbon. The cut-out sugar paste design is made using petal cutters and free-hand stem shapes (see page 87). The colours are applied when the pieces are dry, using blossom tints (see page 54).

Covering a Square Cake Board

1 Once the icing on the cake is completely dry, place the cake on the turntable and make sure the cake board is free from any pieces of dry icing. Spread a thin layer of icing evenly on one side of the cake board. Neaten the edge of the board with a palette knife.

2 Place the cake on a rigid surface and draw the side scraper across the icing to smooth the surface. Repeat if the finish is not satisfactory. Neaten the edge of the board and then ice the opposite side.

3 Leave to dry for 2 hours or overnight, then repeat to ice the remaining sides in the same way, first making sure the sides of the cake board are clean. Leave to dry.
  Repeat with a second layer of icing to give a smooth finish.

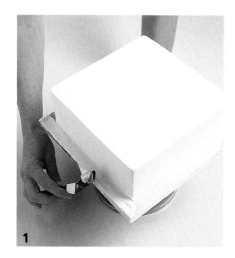

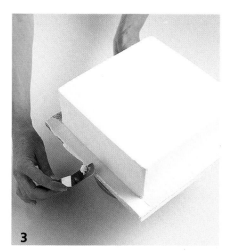

Covering a Round Cake Board

1 Once the icing on the cake is completely dry, place the cake on the turntable and ensure the cake board is free from pieces of dry icing. Spread a thin layer of icing evenly around the cake board.

2 Then, neaten the edge of the board with a palette knife.

3 Holding the side of the cake board and turntable with one hand, place the side scraper on the board with the other hand. Turn the cake and turntable for one complete revolution, pulling the side edge towards you to smooth the icing. Repeat if the finish is not satisfactory.

4 Neaten the edge of the board and leave to dry.
  Repeat with a second layer of icing to give a smooth finish.

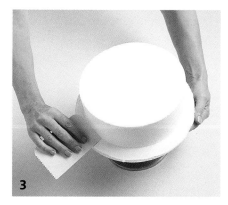

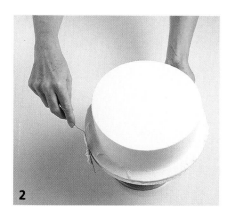

PEAKED ROYAL ICING

Royal icing is very versatile. As well as being smoothed on a cake to give a perfectly flat finish for decorating, it may be peaked and swirled to give a textured finish.

To produce beautifully even peaks, the icing must be of soft-peak consistency. For the best results, peak the side first then the top.

First spread the top and sides of a marzipanned cake evenly with royal icing to obtain a level surface. Smooth the top of the cake by using a straight edge to level the icing and using a side scraper to smooth the icing on the side of the cake so that it is fairly even and completely covers the cake. Ensure the cake board is perfectly clean.

Give the icing a quick stir and make sure the consistency is soft. Dip one side of the blade of a small clean palette knife into the icing. Starting at the base and working to the top edge of the cake, press the palette knife with the icing on the iced cake and pull it sharply away to form a peak. Repeat to form about three or four peaks in a line up the side of the cake, then re-dip the palette knife into the icing and make more peaks in a line down the side of the cake about 1 cm (½ in) along, but staggering the peaks so they don't actually align with adjacent peaks. Continue until the side is completely peaked.

Repeat this process to peak the top of the cake, leaving a smooth area for decorations if desired.

To Make Royal-Icing Peaks

1 Spread one side of the cake with royal icing, and smooth the icing with a side scraper to give a fairly even surface.

2 Press the palette knife dipped in royal icing on the side of the cake. Pull away sharply to form a peak. Repeat to form staggered rows of peaks along the side of the cake. If the icing becomes too messy just smooth it off and start the process again.

Christmas Tree Cake
Peaked royal icing is a classic choice for Christmas cakes with its sparkling crisp texture creating an ice-like effect. This 20 cm (8 in) rich fruit cake is decorated with a cut-out Christmas tree and holly leaves made with special cutters, and also gift-wrapped presents. Use marzipan or sugar paste to make these decorations.

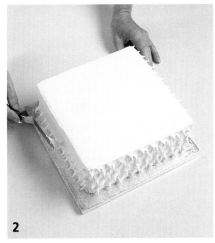

USING FOOD COLOURINGS

The use of colour is vital to any cake design, whether it is a celebration cake covered with delicately tinted sugar paste and decorated with true-to-life flower-paste flowers, or a festive creation with brightly moulded marzipan decorations. A very comprehensive range of good-quality concentrated food colourings is now available from specialist cake-icing and decorating shops. Found as pastes, powders and liquids, each type has its own use for colouring, tinting, painting, brushing on colour, or stencilling.

PASTE AND LIQUID COLOURINGS

Modern food colourings are very concentrated, so they need to be added in small quantities on the tip of a cocktail stick (toothpick) to tint the icing carefully to a delicate shade or a rich, vibrant colour. Every shade is available and, being so concentrated, the consistencies of icing, marzipan or sugar paste are not affected. The colours are also very durable and do not fade. They may also be blended to obtain other colours or shades.

Types of Food Colourings
1 Liquid colourings
2 Dusting brushes
3 Mixing palette
4 Lustre colours
5 Blossom tints
6 Coloured sugar paste decorations
7 Food colouring pens
8 Sugar paste plaque decorated with food colouring pens
9 Paste colourings

When using these food colourings, remember that when added to icings or kneaded into marzipan or sugar paste, the colour may deepen or lighten on drying. Whenever possible, colour icings in the daylight and leave them for at least 15 minutes before initially assessing the colour. As these colours change quite dramatically when they are dry, make samples of coloured icing and leave them to dry before matching the colour of a fabric or flowers to the icing.

At one time food colourings were only available as liquids in a range of primary colours. These are still available from most supermarkets and shops and are adequate for tinting icings, frostings, butter icing, marzipan and sugar paste. With careful blending, other colours and shades can also be achieved. These colourings are, however, fairly diluted so they are only suitable for quite light colours; several spoonfuls of colouring would have to be used for strong, rich colours which will dilute the consistency of the icing, marzipan and sugar paste considerably.

Colouring Butter Icing

1 Butter icing will take more food colouring as fat-based icings do not colour as readily as sugar-based ones. Add the food colouring to the icing using a cocktail stick (toothpick).

2 Beat the butter icing to blend the food colouring evenly throughout the mixture. Add more food colouring if the colour is not deep enough.

Colouring Royal Icing

1 Royal icing will take colour very quickly; so take care to add the colouring drop by drop. Make the royal icing to the consistency required and add the food colouring on the tip of a cocktail stick (toothpick).

2 Mix the food colouring into the royal icing, using a wooden spoon, until the icing is evenly coloured. Add more food colouring if necessary.

Colouring Marzipan

1 Being oil-based, as it contains ground almonds, marzipan will take more food colouring to obtain deeper shades of colour. Add the food colouring to the marzipan using a cocktail stick (toothpick).

2 Knead the marzipan until the colour is evenly distributed throughout and the correct colour has been obtained.

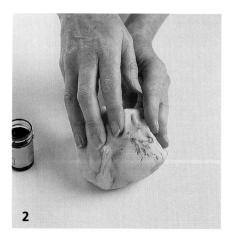

Bunny Big Ears
A brightly coloured cake for a young person's birthday. Butter ice a 20 cm (8 in) square sponge cake and pipe the edges with swirls of butter icing. Top each swirl with alternate beads of black, green and red sugar paste. Roll out a piece of white sugar paste and cover it with alternating strips of red, black and green sugar paste. Cut out the shape with a cookie cutter.

Collage Cake
The design is made up of two basic shapes of dried sugar paste painted with bright, clear paste colours to create an interesting pattern. Match the ribbon to the cut-out sugar pieces and this makes an ideal birthday cake.

Painting Sugar Pieces

1 Make sure the sugar paste pieces are dry. Using a fine paint brush and food colouring paste, paint each piece until evenly coloured.

2 Using a fine paint brush and liquid food colouring, paint the oak leaves slightly unevenly to give a more realistic finish.

3 Arrange the dry coloured sugar pieces as a border pattern to decorate a 20 cm (8 in) round cake covered with sugar paste.

Evenly coloured butter icing, royal icing, marzipan and sugar paste, ready to use.

Colouring Sugar Paste

1 This icing will colour easily so take care when adding the colour. Add the food colouring drop by drop using a cocktail stick (toothpick).

2 Knead the icing with your fingertips to incorporate the food colouring evenly throughout the icing, adding more colouring if it is required.

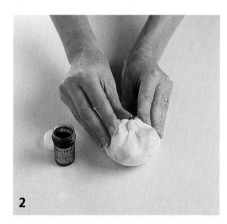

MARBLING SUGAR PASTE

As an alternative to a plain-tinted base covering, try marbling sugar paste with one or several colours. The effect can be subtle or dramatic.

Marbling with One Colour

1 Using a cocktail stick (toothpick), dip it into a food colouring paste. Insert the cocktail stick into the sugar paste so that the colour penetrates into the centre. Repeat to insert the colour about 8 times.

2 Turn the ball of sugar paste over so the coloured marks are underneath and roll out the sugar paste thinly revealing the marbled design.

3 Support the sugar paste over a rolling pin and unroll over the cake to cover evenly.

4 Using lightly cornfloured (cornstarched) palms, smooth the sugar paste evenly over the cake to obtain a smooth and even finish.

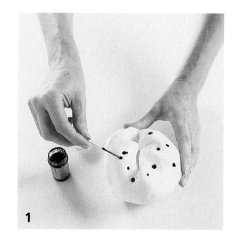

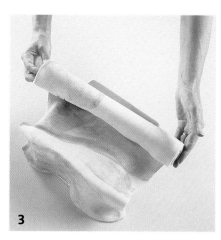

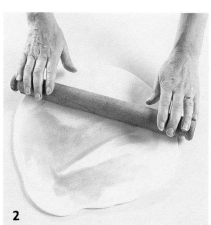

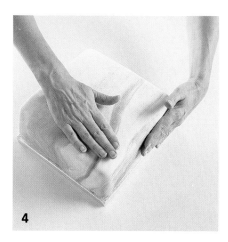

Marbling with Three Colours

1 Roll each coloured piece of sugar paste into a sausage shape. Cut each piece in half and press the alternating colours together.

2 Press the pieces of sugar paste together and roll into one long sausage shape. Fold the sausage shape into three.

3 Roll out the sugar paste thinly enough to cover the cake.

4 A petal-shaped cake board and cake covered with marbled sugar paste ready for decoration.

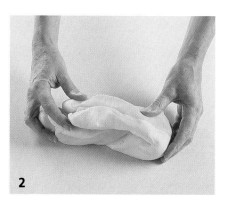

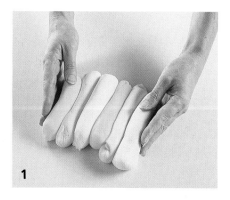

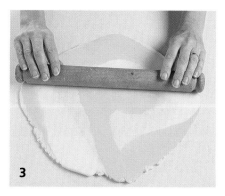

Marbled Cake
A petal-shaped cake covered with tricoloured marbled sugar paste makes a bright birthday or special occasion cake. The frilled plaque is made from sugar paste decorated with plunger blossom flowers and the name written with a food colouring pen. To colour the plaque, brush the edges with petal dust.

BLOSSOM TINTS

Also known as petal dusts, these powdered colours can be brushed or 'dusted' on to moulded and cut-out flowers, sugar pieces and moulded decorations, and can even be applied to cake surfaces. They are always applied when the icing or sugar paste is absolutely dry, which is particularly useful for last-minute work, if matching colours to fresh flowers in season, for example. It also gives you a free hand to add a touch of colour to the finished item and prevents the risk of colour running into the icing when the atmosphere is damp, which may happen when paste colours are used.

Available in a wide range of colours, blossom tints are especially suitable for blending, either in a palette or by applying different colours directly to the finished item, one on top of the other. Blossom tints are also permanent and hold their colour without fading. Available only from cake-icing and decorating specialists, although expensive, they are well worth having simply because they last for so long.

LUSTRE COLOURS AND METALLIC COLOURINGS

Lustre colours are a separate range of colourings for specialized work and are available in gold, silver and a mixture of primary colours. All the colours contain sparkle or glitter, giving a golden or silvered sheen – especially useful for festive decorations. All lustre colours come in a powdered form and need first to be mixed with clear alcohol, such as gin or vodka, before being applied to the dried sugar paste or icing.

Liquid gold and silver colours need to be used according to the manufacturer's instructions. Care must also be taken only to use non-toxic versions of these colours. Gold leaf may also be used for decoration, but it is extremely expensive. Available as 24-carat gold leaf in a tiny container, it must be applied with great care, leaf by leaf, and the decorations must be removed before the cake is cut since gold leaf is inedible. However, the finished result can look stunning on a special celebration cake.

Springtime Cake
An oval cake delicately topped with cut-out sugar paste flowers and leaves would be suitable for a spring birthday, Mother's Day or anniversary cake.

The sugar-paste flowers and leaves are cut out using various cutters and dried completely before colouring. The flowers are tinted with a blend of differently coloured blossom tints and lustre colours to give a more realistic appearance. The leaves are painted unevenly with green liquid food colouring for a realistic finish.

Dusting with Blossom Tints

1 Choose the powdered colours required to colour the flowers and place a little of each in a palette. Using a dusting brush, brush the dry sugar flowers, blending the colours to give a realistic effect.

2 Using a dusting brush, brush these tiny sugar flowers with varying shades of pink and purple.

3 The effect is both attractive and surprisingly realistic.

FOOD COLOURING PENS

These pens look like fibre-tip pens but are filled with edible food colourings. They come in a whole range of bright primary colours as well as black, brown and purple. Food colouring pens have innumerable uses, especially for quick decorating, writing or applying details to models or sugar pieces, and are a must for your cake-decorating collection.

Simply use them like a pen to write a name or message or draw a design on dry royal-icing run-outs, small sugar plaques or even to mark a design directly on an iced cake, taking care not to make mistakes.

Using Food Colouring Pens

1 On a dry sugar paste plaque, use a liquorice food colouring pen to draw the free-hand design.

2 Using red and green food colouring pens, colour in the strawberries and strawberry stems and leaves.

3 Colour in the last leaf to complete the whole design.

Summer Cake
This strawberry design is hand-painted on to a sugar paste plaque and the wild strawberries and leaves are made from sugar paste. This design looks bright on the crisp, clean lines of the royal-iced cake. Write a name or message in the centre of the plaque for a very special birthday or celebration cake.

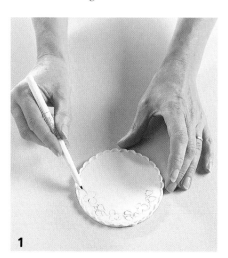

1

2

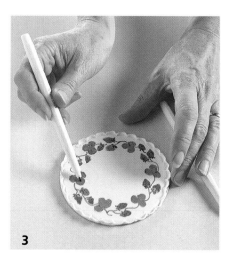

3

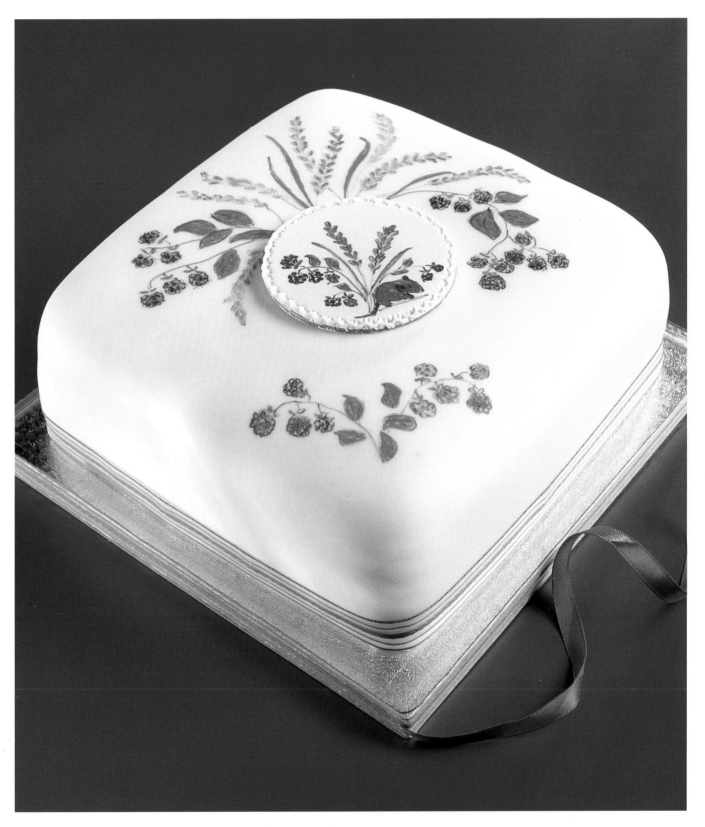

Autumn Cake
This makes a really unusual cake for an autumn birthday or wedding anniversary. The sugar paste plaque is made separately and the design *completed with food colouring pens. Once the sugar paste is dry, lightly draw the free-hand design on the cake with a black food colouring pen, then colour in the details.*

INSTANT DECORATIONS

There are many ways to finish cakes and gâteaux by simply using everyday ingredients found in any store cupboard, such as icing (confectioners') sugar, cocoa and coffee, citrus fruit zest, crystallized (candied) and glacé fruits, and nuts of all descriptions. In addition, there are endless varieties of commercial decorations neatly packaged to provide the finishing touches to a simple cake, such as sugar flowers, sweets (candies), marzipan fruits, jelly diamonds, angelica and dragées.

Types of Instant Decorations

 1 Pecan nuts
 2 Pistachio nuts
 3 Hazelnuts
 4 Orange, lemon and lime zest, cut into strips and made into cut-outs
 5 Mint chocolate sticks
 6 M&Ms
 7 Jelly diamonds
 8 Almonds
 9 Chocolate flake
10 Orange and lemon sweets (candies)
11 Sugar flowers
12 Marzipan fruits
13 Sugared orange and lemon slices
14 Coloured dragées
15 Green and red cherries
16 Glacé fruits
17 Angelica

QUICK-AND-EASY DECORATING

For simple teatime cakes or for when time is at a premium, elaborate sugar paste or marzipan decorations are probably inappropriate. Instead, look in your store cupboard for ready-to-hand decorations and always keep a range of commercial decorations in stock.

ICING (CONFECTIONERS') SUGAR

This simple ingredient, when used carefully, can transform the appearance of a cake. Simply dusting the surface of a sponge cake with icing sugar makes it more appealing. Try placing a patterned doily or arranging 1 cm (½ in) wide strips of paper in lines or in a lattice pattern on top of the cake, then dredge it thickly with icing sugar. Carefully remove the doily or paper strips, revealing the patterned decoration. This looks even more effective when used on a chocolate or coffee cake.

COCOA OR COFFEE

Cocoa or powdered coffee may be used in a similar way to icing (confectioners') sugar to obtain a strong contrast on a light-coloured cake, white icing or cream-finished gâteaux. Mix cocoa or coffee with a little icing sugar and use as described above.

To produce a decorative lattice design, dip a skewer or cocktail stick (toothpick) into cocoa or coffee, then press it on the surface of an iced cake to transfer lines of cocoa or coffee.

CITRUS FRUITS

Oranges, lemons and limes are very versatile and offer effective edible decorations either in the form of the whole sliced fruit, or as segments or simply the zest.

Cut the fruit into wedges, segments or slices – with or without the rind – and use these to decorate cakes or gâteaux. Citrus slices are even more appealing dipped into melted chocolate or caramel.

Citrus zest, when cut into thin strips using a zester or cannelle knife, can transform the appearance of a simply iced cake with a fine shred border. Alternatively arrange it on top of cream whirls. Cut thin strips of lemon, orange or lime zest from the fruits, taking care not to lift up the white pith. Use tiny aspic or cocktail cutters to cut out various shapes. Arrange these shapes on glacé- or butter-iced cakes to form flowers, stems and leaves. Alternatively make a continuous border design using lots of the same shape of cut-out zest but in different colours.

GLACÉ OR CRYSTALLIZED (CANDIED) FRUITS

These traditional decorations are always a good stand-by and can give a very pretty finish to a cake. Angelica may be cut into stem, leaf and diamond shapes. Glacé cherries in various colours can be used whole, cut into halves or thin wedges and arranged as petal shapes to make flowers, or cut into slices and used in a border design. Crystallized fruit, although very expensive, makes a colourful finish to a rich or plain cake. Slice the fruit thinly and arrange the colourful slices in various designs over the top of the cake, then brush with apricot glaze to give a glossy finish.

NUTS

Nuts of all kinds are also very versatile as a quick decoration. Whole assorted nuts arranged over the top of a cake and glazed with honey or sugar syrup look very tempting. Nuts dipped in caramel or melted dark or white chocolate also make a quick decoration for a cake. Chopped nuts are invaluable for coating the sides of iced cakes or creamy gâteaux to give a professional-looking finish.

Icing Sugar
The simplest of decorations for a quick-and-easy sponge cake, this is an attractive finish for when time is at a premium. Arrange strips of evenly spaced paper over the cake top and dredge with icing (confectioners') sugar. Remove the paper strips carefully to avoid blurring the crisp white lines of sugar.

Hedgehog
Such fun for younger people, watch how quickly the hedgehog 'spines' disappear! Simply made with a 20 cm (8 in) round sponge cake, cut in half *to make two semi-circles, the semi-circles are sandwiched together and covered with chocolate butter icing, shaping the face with a palette knife. Short lengths of flaky chocolate sticks* *are pressed evenly all over the cake, and the eyes and nose are made from marzipan. The grated green marzipan covering the board looks so realistic to sit the hedgehog on.*

COMMERCIAL DECORATIONS

Ready-made edible and non-edible decorations are instant and are always worth having as stand-bys. Used carefully, or teamed with other decorations, they can give a very pretty finish to a simple cake. Sugar flowers, jelly diamonds, crystallized (candied) flower petals and marzipan fruits can be used either on top of swirls of icing or pressed on the edge of a cake to make a border pattern, or even simply to decorate iced fancies. Coloured dragées, mimosa balls, hundreds and thousands, and chocolate and coloured sugar strands all make quick and colourful coatings, toppings and designs which are especially appealing on children's birthday cakes or fun novelty cakes.

SWEETS

Always a favourite for children's cakes, these come in all shapes, colours and sizes. White and dark chocolate buttons, yogurt-coated nuts and raisins, jelly beans, jellies, chocolate beans and liquorice sweets can all be used for simple finishes and decorations on party, novelty or simple tea-time cakes.

CARAMEL

This is such an easy and useful medium – the only ingredients needed are sugar and water! Caramel has many uses: it can be drizzled to form abstract shapes for decorations, or used for dipping fruits and nuts to give a wonderful glossy coating which looks like glass.

If caramel is allowed to set into hard sheets (in a baking sheet lined with a piece of lightly oiled foil), it can then be broken into pieces or crushed with a rolling pin and used to coat the sides of an iced cake or gâteau. Praline is a delicious alternative to plain crushed caramel and can be used in exactly the same way.

Happy Bean Cake
Brightly coloured chocolate beans cover this simple butter-iced cake – *ideal for a great instant birthday cake. Use it for a game by counting the different coloured sweets.*

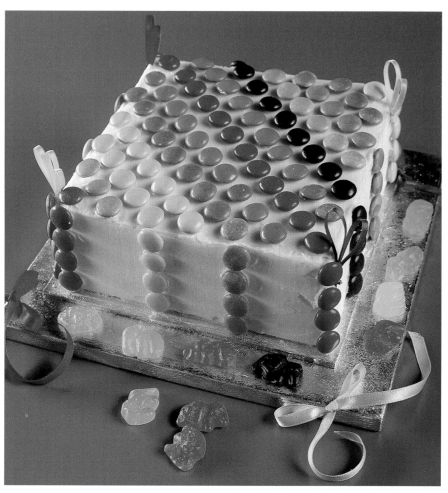

Praline

1 Line a baking sheet with a piece of foil and brush lightly with oil. Toast 75 g (3 oz/½ cup) almonds or hazelnuts until golden brown. Make the caramel (see page 150), and when the bubbles subside add the warm toasted nuts.

2 Carefully shake the pan to mix well, then pour the mixture thinly over the oiled foil and leave to set. Peel off the foil and crush the caramel and nuts finely with a rolling pin to make coarse praline. Alternatively, break into pieces and process in a food processor until finely ground.

Caramel can be used to make or enhance a wide variety of decorations. A few are shown here, including dipped fruits, dipped nuts and abstract caramel shapes.

Praline Gateau
Ideal to serve with coffee or tea, or even suitable for a birthday cake, this 20 cm (8 in) square Genoese cake is covered with butter icing and the top is patterned with a palette knife. Crushed praline coats the side, and the top edges are piped with swirls of icing and decorated with abstract caramel pieces. Placed in the centre of the cake is an arrangement of caramel-dipped physalis.

Abstract Shapes and Dipping Nuts

1 Using a teaspoon, drizzle threads of caramel on lightly oiled foil to make small abstract shapes. If the caramel begins to set, warm the saucepan over a gentle heat until it begins to melt again. When the shapes are set, lift them off carefully and use for decorations.

Dip individual nuts into caramel and place on lightly oiled foil to set. Use whole to decorate cake tops.

Dipping Fruit

1 Use small pieces of dry fruit – such as cherries, grapes, strawberries, berries and kumquats – and dip them into the caramel. Allow to set on a piece of oiled foil.

Caramel-dipped fruit make attractive decorations for cake tops.

USING FLOWERS

Flowers are a natural decoration for a celebration cake. Sugar or flower paste replicas can be made, but although exquisite they do take time. For instant decorations choose fresh or artificial flowers.

FRESH FLOWERS

Fresh flowers seem to be a natural choice to add the finishing touches to a beautifully iced cake. Tiny flowers and leaves positioned at the last minute look so pretty and offer an instant colourful decoration.

Small sprays of fresh flowers or posies are often requested for wedding cakes to match the bridal bouquets. These may be ordered through the wedding florist, but pretty arrangements can also be made at home. Choose small firm flowers such as freesia, Doris pinks, rosebuds, tiny orchids, gypsophila and miniature daisies. Using florists' wire and tape, the individual flowers need to be wired so they can be arranged together before being secured with wire and tape. Ribbons also play an important part in making sprays and posies, and offer pretty shades of colour and contrasting texture.

Making a Fresh Flower Spray

1 Wire the stem of each fresh flower using 10 cm (4 in) lengths of florists' wire.

2 Then bind the wire and stem of each flower with florists' tape.

3 Gather the flowers together into a spray – experiment until you have a pleasing shape and arrangement of flowers. Taking one flower at a time, tape them together, working down the stems until all the flowers are secured.

4 Carefully bend the wires to create a good shape which will sit neatly on top of the cake.

Vary the size, shape and colour of the flowers you select for your arrangement, and experiment with different spray shapes to find one that perfectly complements the overall design of the cake.

Shamrock Cake
This unusual shamrock-shaped rich fruit cake lends itself to many occasions. It may be covered in any shade of sugar paste and trimmed with the appropriate shade of ribbon. The fresh flower arrangement was chosen to complement the colour of the paste and the occasion for which the cake was made.

Hearts and Flowers
A 20 cm (8 in) heart-shaped light fruit cake is covered with marzipan and sugar paste and trimmed with yellow and blue ribbons to match the fresh flower arrangement placed upon it. This design would be suitable for almost any occasion, be it an engagement, anniversary, small wedding or birthday celebration.

SILK FLOWERS

These artificial flowers in fact look very real and are available from cake-decorating specialists, departmental stores or florists. They come in a wide range of blooms and sprays and, chosen carefully for colour and size and teamed with ribbons to make them into posies and sprays, they can serve as instant, reuseable decorations on many cakes.

Silk Flower Arrangement

1 Cut off each bloom from the silk sprays and wire them separately on to 10 cm (4 in) lengths of florists' wire.

2 Cover the stem wire of each flower with florists' tape.

3 Arrange the flowers together to form your chosen spray, then tape them securely together with florists' tape.

4 Add ribbon tails (see page 70) to the silk flower arrangement to finish.

SUGAR-FROSTED FLOWERS

These delicate decorations are simply fresh flowers preserved by egg white and sugar. Once completely dry, they will last for several weeks. Teamed with fine colourful ribbons tied into pretty bows, loops and tails, they are ideal for decorating a cake for almost any occasion.

These flowers may also be wired and fashioned into sprays or posies before frosting. Use immediately, or carefully store the flowers between sheets of tissue paper in a box in a warm dry place until they are required for decorating.

Choose fresh simple small flowers with fairly flat petals, such as violets, primroses, tiny daffodils and freesia, and firm herb or fruit leaves. If possible, pick or buy the flowers and leaves just before you need to frost them and ensure they are young blooms.

Method

1 Dry the flowers and leaves with kitchen paper (paper towels), if necessary, and leave a small stem intact if possible. Place some caster (superfine) sugar on a plate or in a bowl. Using a fine paint brush, paint both sides of the flower petals and leaves and the stems with lightly beaten egg white.

2 Spoon the sugar over the flower petals and leaves to coat them evenly on both sides. Carefully shake the flowers to remove any excess sugar and gently arrange the coated petals and leaves on a wire rack covered with kitchen paper.

Store in a warm dry place until dry. To help keep their shape, some flowers and leaves are better dried with the stems upwards and the petals or leaves flat on the paper.

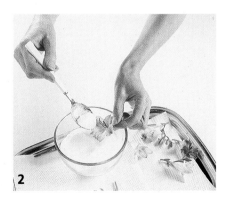

Sugar-Frosted Fruits

1 Fruit can be frosted in the same way as flowers. Choose small fresh fruits in peak condition, such as grapes, cherries, strawberries, lychees, Cape gooseberries, kumquats, and berries. Wipe the fruit so that all surfaces are completely dry. Brush each piece of fruit evenly with lightly beaten egg white.

2 Carefully spoon caster (superfine) sugar over the fruit to cover evenly. Leave to dry on kitchen paper (paper towels) in a warm dry place. Use to decorate cakes or gâteaux, or place in separate paper cases for use as *petits fours*.

Sugar-Frosted Flower Cake
This delicate cake is ideal for a Mother's Day, birthday, anniversary, christening or Easter cake. It is a 20 cm (8 in) round rich fruit cake covered with marzipan and sugar paste. The edge is crimped and the cake and board are trimmed with mauve ribbons and sugar-frosted freesia and minute orchids chosen to match the sugar paste and ribbons.

RIBBONS

Ribbons are invaluable when decorating cakes and cake boards. They are the one non-edible type of decoration which is guaranteed to transform the simplest cake into something quite special.

There are many types of ribbon to choose from, and cake-specialist shops have the widest variety of widths, colours and textures suitable for all types of cake. There are over

Using Ribbons on Cake Boards
Use ribbons to trim cake boards. Choose a ribbon the exact width to match the side of the cake board in a colour to contrast with or complement

100 colours available ranging in width from 2 mm to 5 cm (¹⁄₁₆ in to 2 in) and with plain and fancy edges.

The most popular ribbon for decoration is double-faced polyester satin, used to make bows, loops and tails for cakes and flower sprays. It is also used to band cake boards and to fit around the sides of cakes to match the cake design and colour.

Velvet, nylon, paper and synthetic fabric ribbons found in gift-wrap departments and florists can also be used to great effect. These types of ribbon look pretty around cake boards or used for posies or sprays.

an element of the finished cake. A narrow band of contrasting ribbon can then be pinned on top of the first for an alternative effect. Always use stainless-steel pins.

RIBBON PICTURES

Ribbons can also be used to make simple designs or collages to decorate the top of the cake. Plan the design on paper first, then simply cut the ribbons to size and apply them to the cake. Paint the ends with royal icing to fix the ribbons to the cake's surface. Use ribbons of different textures, widths and colours to make pretty pictures.

Method

1 Cut the various ribbons to length and place them roughly in position, moving the pieces and changing the colours until you are pleased with the design.

2 Secure all the ribbon pieces to the cake surface with royal icing. This ribbon picture has been applied to a sugar paste plaque, so it can be removed and kept as a memento.

BOWS AND LOOPS

These are best made from the narrowest ribbon to produce neat tiny bows which may be attached to the side or top of the cake. They can be teamed with ribbons around the base and top of the cake and give an instant decoration. Loops look lovely wired into sprays of flowers, or just arranged with moulded sugar flowers. Using florists' wire, several shades of ribbons may be wired into fine loops with curled tail ends and arranged on the cake with fresh sugar-frosted, silk or sugar flowers.

Ribbon Loops

For simple and flamboyant loop designs, fold the ribbon into single, double or treble (or more) loops using one or several colours. Secure with florists' wire and finish with florists' tape if needed. Always remember to remove these decorations from the cake before cutting.

Ribbon Bows

Tiny ribbon bows add delicate touches to a cake design and they can be made in various colours and sizes, using different widths of ribbon. Tie the bows neatly — tweezers are sometimes useful for minuscule ones — and trim off the tails to the length required. Curl the tails by pulling the ends over a scissor blade.

Ribbon Tails

Ribbons can also be folded or looped into a variety of shapes to make decorative ribbon tails. Secure the loops into position with beads of royal icing and decorate the ribbon surface.

Ribbon Picture Cake

This 20 cm (8 in) rich fruit cake is covered with marzipan and sugar paste and would be suitable for numerous occasions. The sugar paste plaque is simply decorated with ribbons cut to length to make a flower pot full of flowers.

DECORATING WITH CHOCOLATE

Chocolate comes in many forms, depending on the way it is processed. It may be found as milk, plain (semi-sweet) and white chocolate bars and dots, as thick richly flavoured spreads, as cocoa powder (unsweetened cocoa) or drinking chocolate, or even distilled into smooth liqueurs. It is a luxury ingredient and a highly processed and expensive product, so great care must be taken when using it. Be sure to choose the right chocolate and follow the guidelines to obtain the best results.

CHOOSING CHOCOLATE

Choosing chocolate for cake decoration can be quite daunting, as there are so many varieties and flavours from which to choose. There are basically four grades of chocolate: couverture, cooking chocolate, dessert or eating chocolate, and chocolate-flavoured cake covering.

The ingredient which determines the quality of the chocolate is the cocoa butter, which is extremely expensive. The more cocoa butter contained in the chocolate, the finer the texture and richer the flavour. The original cocoa butter found in chocolate is often replaced with different percentages of vegetable fat, grading the chocolate into different qualities for a variety of uses.

All grades of chocolate are available as milk, plain (semi-sweet) and white chocolate. The plainer the chocolate, the harder the texture and the stronger the flavour. Milk chocolate is milder and sweeter, and white chocolate is sweet with no real distinctive chocolate flavour.

Couverture: is the finest and most expensive chocolate, made entirely with cocoa butter and producing a chocolate of superior quality, flavour and texture. It is available from specialist shops and has to be tempered before use.

Tempering chocolate is a very exacting process. Cocoa butter is an unstable substance made up of a number of individual fats that all melt at different temperatures. To be melted, it has to be heated and cooled to different temperatures before it can be used successfully, so beginners are advised to leave this to more experienced hands.

Cooking chocolate: is a good all-round chocolate suitable for all types of recipe. The quality depends on how much cocoa butter has been retained, and this also affects the flavour, colour and texture of the chocolate. Cooking chocolate is easy to work with and melts readily to a consistency suitable for spreading, coating, dipping and piping.

Dessert or eating chocolate: has a wonderful flavour and refined texture. Being more expensive than cooking chocolate, it is better to select this chocolate for special desserts and gâteaux, sweets and chocolates, or for chocolate decorations.

Chocolate-flavoured cake covering: is widely available, easy to use and less expensive to buy. It can no longer be called chocolate because it has more vegetable fat than cocoa butter, giving a poorer flavour and a rather soft and greasy texture. It may be used for all recipes, but remember the flavour is not going to be as good as that of real chocolate. When melted it goes very liquid and sets quickly. Being soft it is also ideal for quick chocolate curls shaved directly from the block (see pages 80–81).

Types of Chocolate
1 Milk couverture
2 Plain (semi-sweet) cake covering
3 & 14 Milk cake covering
4 & 10 Luxury plain cooking
      chocolate
5 Cocoa powder
6 Plain cooking chocolate
7 White chocolate dots
8 White dessert chocolate
9 Plain dessert chocolate
11 Plain chocolate dots
12 Milk chocolate dots
13 White cake covering

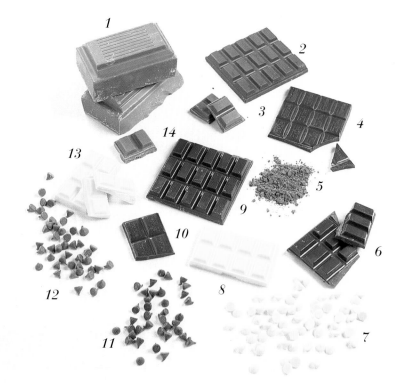

To Melt Chocolate

1 First always use fresh chocolate to ensure a good flavour. Break the chocolate into small pieces and place them in a large clean dry bowl over a saucepan of *hand-hot* water. Ensure the base of the bowl does not touch the water and do not heat the water.

2 Stir the chocolate when it has melted completely. You cannot hurry this process and the chocolate temperature should never exceed 38–43°C (100–110°F), otherwise when it sets the surface will be dull and streaky.

MELTING CHOCOLATE

Melting chocolate is an exacting process if you require the chocolate to set to a smooth glossy appearance. For dipping chocolates, coating biscuits or for cut-out chocolate pieces and decorations, use the method described below.

● Never allow moisture, steam or condensation to come into contact with chocolate or it will become thick and unstable.

● Leave the bowl over the hot water during use, unless you require the chocolate to become thicker.

● For speed, use a microwave cooker to melt the chocolate: place the chocolate pieces in a bowl and heat in the microwave cooker on the lowest setting for 3 to 4 minutes until the chocolate has almost melted, then stir until smooth. Take care that there is no moisture in the microwave left by heating liquids, otherwise this will affect the chocolate when it is melted.

● Any leftover melted chocolate can always be reused so there is no waste. Wrap it in foil to exclude all air and store for up to one month in a cool dry place.

● Any chocolate which has been over-heated during the melting process still remains ideal for use in cakes, desserts and other recipes needing melted chocolate.

Note: White chocolate lends itself to being coloured, especially for decorating or coating assorted chocolates. Use oil-based or powdered food colourings as any liquids added to chocolate will cause it to thicken and become unusable.

White Chocolate Cake
This 20 cm (8 in) chocolate sandwich cake is covered with a smooth layer of butter icing before being coated with melted white chocolate. The top edge is decorated with a shell edging of chocolate and hazelnut spread, and the top and sides are finished with a simple decoration of chocolate cut-out pieces.

Chocolate Fruit Gateau
Two 20 cm (8 in) cakes, one chocolate and one plain, are each split into two layers. Alternate layers are sandwiched together and covered with whipped dairy cream flavoured with melted chocolate. The cake is then completely coated in melted plain (semi-sweet) chocolate to give a luxurious glossy finish, and decorated with chocolate-dipped fresh fruits and chocolate leaves.

USING MELTED CHOCOLATE FOR COATING

Melted chocolate can be used to coat all types of edible items completely or partially.

Whole cakes can be given a glossy covering of chocolate, and small fancies and biscuits can be coated in much the same way. Small items, such as homemade sweets and fruits, can be more easily dipped into a bowl of melted chocolate. Use a confectioners' dipping fork or a large dinner fork for dipping and have several sheets of baking parchment ready to take the dipped items. Always ensure that anything you wish to coat is at room temperature or the chocolate will set before coating smoothly.

Dipping Sweets

1 Dip homemade sweets one at a time into a bowl of melted chocolate using a large fork. Remove and tap the fork to allow the excess chocolate to fall.

2 Leave the dipped sweets to set on a sheet of parchment paper.

Coating a Cake with Chocolate

1 Melt the chocolate in a bowl and check the consistency. Wipe the condensation from the outside of the bowl. Place the cake on a wire cooling rack, over baking parchment.

2 In one movement, tip the bowl of chocolate over the cake so that the chocolate flows over the top and evenly down the sides.

3 Shake the wire rack gently to encourage the chocolate to flow.

Dipping Fruits

1 A selection of colourful fruits, half-dipped in either plain (semi-sweet), milk or white chocolate, looks very appealing. Make sure the fruit is dry and at room temperature.

2 Hold the stalk end of fruit and carefully dip into one of the bowls of chocolate. Gently shake the fruit to allow the excess chocolate to fall.

3 Leave the dipped fruits to set on baking parchment.

Chocolate Leaves

1 From real flowers, herbs and plants, choose leaves which are small, firm and have well-defined veins. Pick the leaves as freshly as possible and dry them thoroughly on kitchen paper (paper towels).

Using a medium-sized paint brush, thickly coat the underside of each leaf with melted chocolate, taking care not to paint over its edge or the leaf will not peel away from the chocolate.

2 Place the leaves on baking parchment, chocolate side uppermost, in a cool place to set. Just before using, peel the real leaves away from the chocolate leaves and discard.

3 Use the chocolate leaves for decorations. They can be made with plain (semi-sweet), milk or white chocolate.

PIPING WITH CHOCOLATE

Melted chocolate is quite difficult to pipe through a metal tube as the coldness of the metal sets the chocolate before it can be piped.

One way round this is to add a few drops of glycerine to the chocolate to thicken it (rather than allow the chocolate to cool and thicken), then pipe this through a tube as quickly as possible. If the chocolate does start to set, warm the piping tube in your hands. If you only need to pipe simple decorative threads or chocolate outlines (for piped chocolate pieces and chocolate run-outs, for example), use a greaseproof-paper piping bag with the end snipped off to a point. Alternatively, and the simplest solution of all, use chocolate and hazelnut spread as this has the ideal consistency.

Always choose simple shapes for off-set piping: stylized flowers work well for piped pieces, and animals, hearts, flowers, bells, horseshoes, numbers or letters are the ideal choices for run-outs. Cookie cutters make excellent templates for these sorts of design.

Using Chocolate Spread

1 Place the chocolate and hazelnut spread in a greaseproof-paper piping bag fitted with a small star tube and use to pipe attractive borders of shells, stars or whirls.

Piped Chocolate Pieces

1 Draw the chosen designs on a piece of paper. Place baking parchment or run-out film over the top of this and secure the corners in place with tape. Fill a greaseproof-paper piping bag with chocolate, fold down the top and snip off the end.

2 Pipe fine threads of chocolate following the outline of the designs, or pipe free-hand designs. Leave to set, then carefully slide a thin palette knife under each piece to loosen it from the paper and use for decorating.

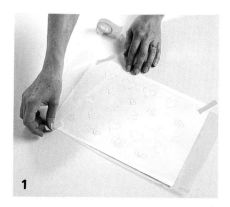

Feathered Gateau
A light whisked 20 cm (8 in) chocolate sponge is cooked in a moule à manqué mould. The cake is split into three layers, filled and covered with whipped dairy cream and then coated with melted plain (semi-sweet) chocolate and feathered with white chocolate. The top is piped with stars of cream and decorated with piped chocolate pieces.

Piping without a Tube

1 For simple lines and threads, take a greaseproof-paper piping bag and snip off the end to whatever size of hole you need. Pipe thin threads of chocolate in straight or zig-zag lines.

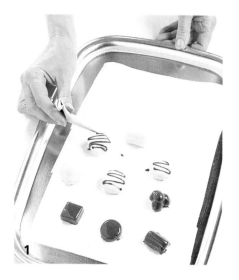

Chocolate Run-Outs

1 Draw or trace the chosen shape several times – to allow for breakages – on a piece of paper. Place a piece of baking parchment or run-out film over the top and secure the edges in place with tape.

2 Using two greaseproof-paper piping bags, half-fill each with melted chocolate and fold down the tops. Snip off the point from one piping bag and pipe a thread of chocolate around the edge of the design. You may achieve better results if you wait for the chocolate to thicken slightly as you will then obtain a clean thread of chocolate.

3 Cut the end off the remaining piping bag and fill in the run-out with melted chocolate so that it looks rounded and over-filled. Leave to set completely.

4 Pipe in any details or design if necessary, then allow to set hard. Carefully peel off the paper and use as cake decorations. These can be prepared in advance and stored.

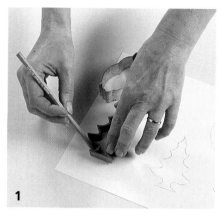

USING PARTIALLY SET CHOCOLATE FOR DECORATIONS

Chocolate which has been melted, formed into thin flat sheets and allowed almost to set can be used in various decorative ways.

By drawing a sharp knife across the chocolate, and varying the angle and pressure, wafer-thin chocolate curls, rolls and frills can be made. Alternatively, plain, fancy and specially shaped cocktail and cookie cutters can be pressed into the pliable chocolate to make instant cut-out decorations.

When making any form of chocolate curl, frill, flake or caraque, the temperature of the set chocolate is all-important. Always allow the chocolate to set at room temperature and keep testing the edge to see if the chocolate is ready to curl: chocolate which is too soft will not curl, and hard-set chocolate is too brittle and will break. Once a good curl forms readily, work quickly and precisely with the chocolate.

To prepare, pour the melted chocolate on a smooth rigid surface, such as a piece of marble, wood or plastic laminate. Spread it evenly backwards and forwards with a palette knife until thinly and evenly spread.

Chocolate Curls, Caraque and Frills

1 Curls: when the chocolate has set, but is not too hard (the temperature is most important as explained above) use a sharp knife held at a 45° angle to the surface of the chocolate with the blade towards you. Draw the knife towards you across the surface to shave off thin layers of chocolate which form into curls. If the chocolate is too soft, it will not curl; if it is too set, it will be brittle and will break.

2 Large curls or caraque: draw a long-bladed knife down the whole length and across the whole width, if desired, of the chocolate to form it into long thin curls. To make loose curls of chocolate, use a side scraper instead of a knife and push it against the chocolate to form loose wide curls.

3 Frills: using a side scraper or knife in the same way as for making chocolate curls, but applying a little more pressure, press the end of the scraper or point of the blade slightly deeper into the chocolate at the top edge. Pull the blade at this tilted angle down the edge of the chocolate just under the surface to form narrow lengths of frilled chocolate. Lift off and set before using.

Chocolate Birthday Cake
Two 20 cm (8 in) chocolate chip sponge cakes are sandwiched together and covered with butter icing. A shell edging is piped around the base and the top edge and decorated with chocolate dots. The sides are decorated with moulded chocolate animals and the top with a chocolate run-out tree.

Chocolate curls, caraque and frills are a lovely textural form of decoration and can be used on both the tops and sides of cakes.

SHAVINGS AND MINI CURLS

● Make chocolate shavings in the same way, but let the chocolate set a little harder and then draw the knife only half-way across the surface to shave off fine flakes.

● To make tiny curls, use a potato peeler to shave the curls off the side of a block of chocolate at room temperature. Chocolate-flavoured cake covering is also just the right texture for curling. Alternatively grate any type of chocolate on a coarse grater.

Chocolate Curl Cake
Two 20 cm (8 in) round chocolate cakes are sandwiched together and coated with chocolate icing, lined on the top with a palette knife. The base and top edge are piped with butter icing, and decorated with small curls of plain (semi-sweet) and white chocolate which can be easily made with a vegetable peeler.

Chocolate Cut-Outs

1 Pour the melted chocolate on a piece of baking parchment, Spread as evenly as possible with a palette knife.

2 Pick up and drop the corners of the paper a few times to level the chocolate and remove air bubbles from it.

3 When the chocolate can be touched without it sticking to the fingers, carefully peel off the backing paper.

4 To cut out squares or triangles: carefully measure and mark the size of the squares required. Using a fine sharp knife or scalpel and the straight edge of a ruler, cut along the marked lines and remove the shapes. Cut squares diagonally in half for triangles.

5 To cut out shapes: press any shaped cocktail, biscuit, plain or fluted cutters on the chocolate and cut out and remove the shapes, working quickly while the chocolate is pliable. (Once it sets too hard, it becomes brittle and the shapes may break.)

6 Leave the cut-outs in a cool place to set hard before using.

Chocolate Curl Gâteau
This rich gâteau is made with two 23 cm (9 in) round chocolate sponge cakes. The cakes are sandwiched together and covered with chocolate butter icing. The sides are evenly coated with grated plain (semi-sweet) chocolate, and the top is decorated with long chocolate curls and frills giving a dramatic result.

DECORATING WITH SUGAR PASTE AND MARZIPAN

There are many uses for sugar paste other than simply covering cakes. This pliable paste may be cut out, moulded, frilled, crimped, embossed and used in many other exciting ways.
Marzipan is also smooth, soft and easy to work and can be cut into shapes or moulded into flowers and animal figures. Both mediums may be tinted and coloured in various shades using food colourings, making them ideal for decorative work.

DECORATING CAKE COVERINGS

There are two very useful techniques which provide an instant way of decorating cakes covered in sugar paste or marzipan: crimping and embossing.

With the first the surface of the cake is literally pinched with a tool rather like large tweezers. These crimpers are available with different shaped and sized end-pieces, producing curved lines, scallops, ovals, 'V'-shapes, hearts, diamonds and zig-zags etc. Embossing tools stamp a design on the cake surface and they are available in a large range of patterns and designs. These items of equipment are available from cake-icing specialists; choose just one or two examples of each initially.

CRIMPING

To polish your technique and to obtain an even crimped design, always practise on a spare piece of sugar paste before working on a cake.

Always crimp on a cake which has been freshly covered with sugar paste or marzipan.

To Crimp a Design

1 Ensure that the crimper is quite clean, then dust it with cornflour (cornstarch) to prevent sticking. Place the crimper on the edge of the cake, then squeeze firmly to mark the sugar paste or marzipan. Gently release and lift off the crimper, taking care it does not spring apart or it will tear the sugar paste or marzipan. Place the crimper next to the marked pattern and then repeat all around the top of the cake, dipping the crimper in cornflour occasionally.

2 Use on the base and sides of various shaped cakes, if wished, or make a design across the top.

EMBOSSING

Many other tools apart from specialized embossers may be used to impress a pattern into the sugar paste, such as spoon handles, tops of icing tubes, or anything small with a defined pattern.

Colour may be added by painting part or all of the design with food colouring using a fine brush. Petal dust or food colouring pens may also be used when the sugar paste is dry. Dipping the embossing tool into coloured petal dust will imprint the pattern with the colour and give a very professional look.

Choose the design you wish to emboss on to the cake. First practise on a small piece of sugar paste to create the design before embarking on the cake. Try various methods of col-

ouring the design, either by painting with food colours, colouring with food colouring pens, or using petal dust with the embossing tool.

To Emboss a Pattern

1 Ensure the cake is freshly covered in sugar paste and dust the embossing tool with cornflour (cornstarch) or petal dust, if you want colour. Take care to press the embossing tool into the sugar paste to the same depth and at the same angle each time, to give an even design.

2 Dust with cornflour or petal dust each time to prevent sticking or to imprint the colour, and continue around the cake until the design is complete.

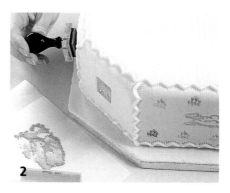

Monogram Cake
An unusual shaped cake which would be ideal for a retirement or 21st birthday cake. The embossed and crimped designs are quick to do, and the colours may be determined by the blossom tints or lustre colours used. Choose a rubber stamp with the initials required, and a patterned shape for the remaining sides. An arrangement of silk flowers and ribbons complete the decoration.

CUT-OUT DECORATIONS

There are a vast range of cutters to make cut-out decorations: cookie cutters, aspic or cocktail cutters, garrette cutters for frills, and specialized flower and leaf cutters in many designs. Alternatively, use homemade card templates to cut around for your own designs. Following a few simple techniques, it is a simple method of making attractive decorations; the skill comes in applying the pieces to the cake surface, which can be fiddly – but the results are well worth the effort.

MARZIPAN AND SUGAR PASTE CUT-OUTS

Simple cut-outs make an instant decoration for any iced cake. If wished, first colour the sugar paste or marzipan in your chosen colours, kneading each piece lightly until evenly coloured (see pages 48 and 51). Then, on a surface lightly dusted with sieved icing (confectioners') sugar, roll it out thinly until about 3 mm (⅛ in) thick. Use your chosen cutters to cut out a number of shapes.

Always leave sugar paste cut-outs to dry before applying to the cake surface with egg white or royal icing. Alternatively – especially if a large number of cut-out pieces are needed to decorate a large cake or several tiers – they can also be made in advance and stored in a box in a warm, dry place until required. Marzipan cut-outs should be applied directly to the cake and secured in place with apricot glaze.

Use the cut-outs to form an attractive border or side decoration. Alternatively, make a flower design for the top of a cake using small flower or leaf cutters, cutting stems from thin strips and marking the leaf veins with a knife. Leaves can also be dried curved over a piece of dowelling for a three-dimensional effect.

For a truly individual cut-out decoration, design a picture and cut out a template as a guide (look at greetings cards or wallpaper designs for inspiration). Cut out the individual components of the picture from coloured marzipan or sugar paste and assemble them on the cake, building up the shapes. Once the picture has been assembled, secure each piece and mark in any details using food colouring pens.

Making Cut-Outs

1 Roll the sugar paste or marzipan thinly. Use a variety of small cutters to cut out as many shapes as you need to complete the design.

2 Arrange the shapes to form a border, side decoration or top design, securing the sugar paste pieces with royal icing and the marzipan ones with apricot glaze.

Christening Cake
A 20 cm (8 in) oval rich fruit cake covered with marzipan and sugar paste makes an ideal shape for a christening cake. The cut-out sugar paste hearts and blossoms may be pink or blue, and are quick to make using plunger cutters. The bib is made from flower paste and has a broderie anglaise design with the name piped across the bib. This may be kept as a memento of the occasion.

SUGAR PIECES AND EXTENSIONS

Delicate sugar pieces may be cut out of sugar paste and left for several days to dry. However, extension pieces are best made from flower paste (see page 148) as they need to dry quickly, be fine and yet strong as generally they are attached to the edges of the cake to extend the design. Many wonderful shapes may be created from sugar or flower paste using cutters, icing-tube tips and crimpers, so work out the design first. Make a few test pieces and try them on the iced cake so that you can work out how many pieces are required. Tint the paste a pale shade, or leave it the original colour and dust the pieces with blossom tints (or petal dust) when they are dry.

Method

1 Roll out the sugar or flower paste in small quantities (flower paste dries particularly quickly). Roll it so thinly that you can almost see through it. Using cutters of varying shapes and sizes, or a template, cut out as many pieces from the rolled-out paste as you can. Arrange these pieces on a flat surface dusted with cornflour (cornstarch) or on a piece of foam sponge and leave in a warm, dry place until hard. Repeat this procedure to make the number of extensions or sugar pieces needed to decorate the cake.

2 When they are all dry, tint them with blossom tints, if wished, and arrange them roughly on the cake to

Doily Cake

Cut-out filigree sugar pieces, attached to the base and top of this cake, give the effect of a doily design. The cut-out pieces from the plunger heart cutters are also used on the top and side of the cake. This sharp, clear design enhances the sharp lines of a royal-iced cake, and the name may be added to the centre making this a suitable christening cake.

ensure the design fits properly. Attach the sugar pieces to the cake with royal icing and allow them to dry overnight in a covered box in a warm dry place.

3 Remember to use a large cake board when fitting extension pieces on to the cake, otherwise the design will look unbalanced and breakages will occur when the cake is boxed.

CUT-OUT AND APPLIQUÉD DESIGNS

This is a very clever way of decorating an entirely plain iced cake with a cut-out sugar paste or marzipan design which covers the top and sides of the cake. Designs from many sources may be used, but the most inspiring designs come from fabric patterns, wallpaper prints or paper-pattern embroidery designs.

Once the cake has been covered with sugar paste and the design has been selected, trace the detail on greaseproof paper to make a complete template. Select the colours for the chosen design and tint the sugar paste or marzipan accordingly. Alternatively, leave the sugar paste or marzipan in the original colour and paint the food colours on when the design has been cut out.

Dust the work surface with icing (confectioners') sugar and roll out the sugar paste or marzipan thinly. Using a small sharp knife or scalpel, cut out the design pieces. Colour the pieces, if necessary, and apply them one by one to the cake, taking care not to over-handle or distort the pieces. Press them gently in position to make up the design.

Another method is to knead equal parts of flower paste and sugar paste together so that the sugar paste design sets hard before applying the design to the cake. The advantage of this is that the pieces may be applied so that they stand proud of the cake, or pieces may be set at an angle, holding their own shape to give a three-dimensional appearance to the cake.

Accuracy of the designs is all-important to this method of decorating a cake as the cake has a very graphic appearance and any mistakes are very noticeable.

Appliqué Design

1 Trace the design on a piece of greaseproof paper.

2 Roll out the coloured sugar paste thinly, place the pattern on top of the sugar paste and mark the design with a pin or marker.

3 Cut out the marked design on the sugar paste using a scalpel or sharp knife.

4 Arrange the cut-out pieces on the paper design to ensure they fit before marking out the remaining design pieces.

5 Place the sugar pieces carefully in position on the cake, checking before finally securing them with a little egg white or royal icing.

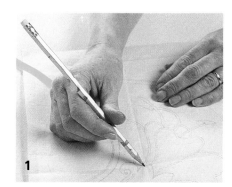

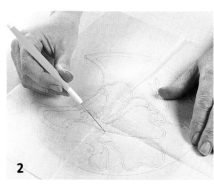

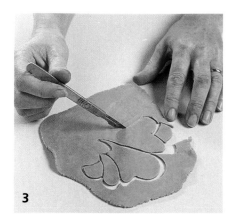

Appliqué Cake

This simple floral design, taken from a furnishing fabric, has been transformed into a stunning sugar paste design on a round white sugar paste cake. It is a cake suitable for many occasions, especially for someone who appreciates flowers and design. Use any 20 cm (8 in) base cake covered with marzipan and sugar paste as a base for the design.

ADVANCED SUGAR PASTE DECORATIONS

The following decorating techniques – frills and flounces, ribbon insertion, and broderie anglaise – will require a little more time and patience to master. However, the finished effects are quite stunning and will be the focal decorative touch to any special celebration cake.

The following instructions will lead you carefully through each stage, but do practise the techniques on dummy cakes or using sugar paste trimmings until you are completely satisfied with the results and feel ready to embark on the real article.

FRILLS AND FLOUNCES

These look spectacular when attached to a cake of any shape, either in single layers, in several layers, in scalloped or arched designs or simply attached to the base of the cake to cover the cake board.

Their appearance may be further enhanced by crimping (see page 85) the edge of the frill where it is attached to the cake, piping details above and below the frills, embossing the top edge of the frill (see page 86), or by incorporating ribbon insertion designs (see page 94).

Frills may be made from sugar paste as this frills readily. Sugar paste frills do, however, have a tendency to drop if they are applied too quickly. It is advisable to knead one part of flower paste into two parts sugar paste, so that the frills set more quickly. Alternatively, knead ½ teaspoon of gum tragacanth into 225 g (8 oz) sugar paste about 24 hours before use.

Tint the sugar paste with food colouring to the required colour, or brush the dry frills with blossom tints to achieve a softer effect.

Always apply sugar paste frills to a cake that has been covered with sugar paste the day before so that the cake is not marked while applying the frills.

To Make Frills

1 On a surface lightly dusted with cornflour (cornstarch), roll out a small piece of sugar paste thinly and evenly until you can almost see through it. Cut out a 7.5 cm (3 in) round using a fluted cutter. Then, using a 4 cm (1½ in) plain cutter, cut out and remove the centre of the round. Alternatively you could use a garrette cutter which is especially made for cutting out frills. Make sure the sugar paste is not sticking to the surface.

2 Place the end of a cocktail stick (toothpick) sprinkled with cornflour on the outer edge of the circle. Roll the cocktail stick backwards and forwards along the edge of each flute with the fingers until the edge of the icing begins to frill. Continue this process to move round the edge of the icing until the edge is completely frilled.

3 Cut the ring open with a sharp knife, then gently ease the frill open. Turn the frill over so the neat side shows.

4 Using a paper template (see page 15), scribe a line on the cake side to mark the position and drop for the first frill.

5 Pipe a line of royal icing following the shape where the frill has to be attached.

6 Press the frill gently in position and trim to achieve a perfect fit if this is necessary. ▶

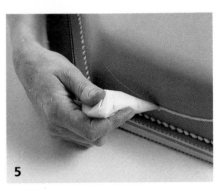

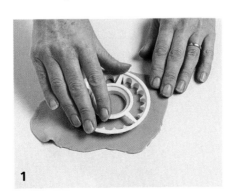

7 Lift the base of the frill slightly with a plastic modelling tool, if necessary, so it stands away from the cake side.

8 Repeat this procedure to attach more frills round the cake. If wished, add extra layers above the frills already attached to make a multi-frilled design. Finish the top edge of the frill with a crimper or embossing tool.

9 Inverted frills are an attractive alternative giving a 'ruffled' appearance. The method for making and applying is exactly the same.

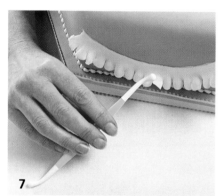

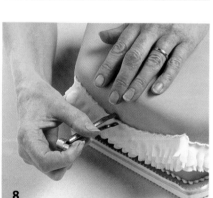

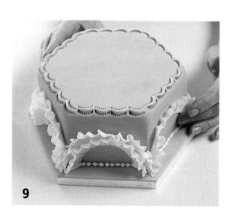

Wedgwood Cake

This is ideal for a single-tiered wedding cake or an anniversary cake. The hexagonal shape lends itself to the scalloped sugar paste frills finished with a crimped edge and decorated with a tiny cut-out sugar paste heart border. The top is *decorated with a small arrangement of silk flowers held together with ribbon. The cake is a 25 cm (10 in) rich fruit cake covered with marzipan and blue sugar paste. A tiny shell border is piped from a No 3 plain writing tube before the frills are applied.*

TO MAKE A FRILLED PLAQUE

Colour the sugar paste, if wished, and roll it out thinly on a surface dusted with cornflour (cornstarch). Cut out the shape and size of the plaque required using an oval, square or round plain or fluted cutter. Frill the edge using a cocktail stick (toothpick) as described before. Leave the plaque on a flat surface or foam sponge to dry. Dust the plaque with petal dust to colour, if wished, and pipe with royal icing to decorate. Alternatively, use food colouring pens to write on the plaque and to add the design or border.

Peach Wedding Cake
Softly frilled champagne sugar paste is the main feature of this simple but beautiful cake decorated with peach-coloured plunger blossom flowers, ribbons and bows. The fresh flower arrangement complements beautifully the delicate colouring of the ribbons and sugar paste. Just the top tier of the cake is shown here.

RIBBON INSERTION

This technique creates the effect of a single piece of ribbon having been threaded through the sugar paste. The design can be straight, diagonal or curved and combined with crimper work or dainty piping to make it an even more special feature.

The cake should be freshly covered with sugar paste and should feel firm on the surface, but soft underneath.

It is important to work out the design very accurately using a template to make the insertions into the sugar paste, as it is very noticeable if the ribbon insertions are uneven.

First choose the colour and width of the ribbon required to match the shape and colour of the cake. Then plan the design on paper, making sure it is accurate. Cut as many pieces of ribbon as are needed to complete the design. The ribbon pieces should be slightly larger than the spaces allowed, leaving enough excess to tuck either end into the icing.

Method

1 Using a stainless-steel pin or scribing tool, mark the design accurately on the freshly sugar-pasted cake.

2 Using a very fine blade or scalpel, cut the slits accurately in the icing following the lines you have already marked.

3 Carefully insert one end of the piece of ribbon into a slit using a pin or fine blade.

4 Then tuck the other end of the ribbon into the next slit in the same way. Press gently to neaten. Leave a space and repeat to insert another piece of ribbon until all the slits are filled. Finish off the ribbon insertion with tiny bows, fine piping or crimping.

Nicola's Cake
This dainty design shows how ribbon insertion and piped embroidery can enhance a square cake. The ribbon is inserted on the top and sides of the
cake using a round and straight template. The bead and line design and the name are piped in white from a No 1 plain writing tube, then over-piped in green icing to match the
ribbons. The base of the cake and the board are trimmed with matching ribbons. This cake is ideal for a birthday or christening; the colours may be changed to suit the occasion.

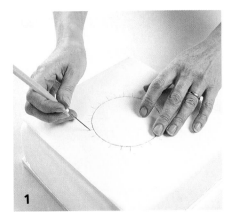

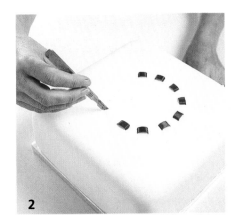

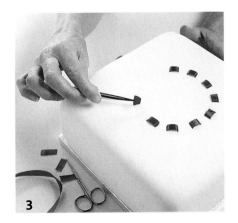

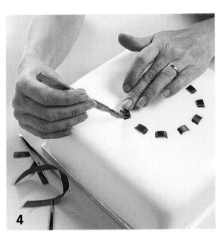

BRODERIE ANGLAISE

This is a most effective way of decorating a cake covered with sugar paste. The dainty design may be applied directly to the cake or made in the shape of a sugar plaque. It looks just like a piece of embroidered cotton lawn and may be worked in white or coloured sugar paste with contrasting piping.

Designs and patterns may be obtained from paper embroidery patterns or copied from table linen, fabric prints or porcelain designs. Traditional *broderie anglaise* has a scalloped edge neatened with a button-hole stitch or *petit point*. This can be interpreted using a No 0 piping tube and royal icing, marking out the pattern using a knitting needle.

The pricking out of the pattern must be accurate and great care taken not to lean on the sugar paste, or the surface will be spoiled.

To make a template: work out the size of the plaque to fit the cake which is being decorated; this should be about 2.5 cm (1 in) smaller than the top of the cake. Cut out a paper template. Draw and mark the design accurately on the paper template, ensuring there are an even number of scallops as follows: fold the round paper template in half several times to form a narrow cone shape. Draw a semi-circle at the broad end of the cone and cut around the shape to make the scalloped edge. Open up the template and press flat.

To Make a Broderie Anglaise *Plaque*

1 On a surface lightly dusted with icing sugar, roll out the sugar paste thinly and place it on a cake board which also has been dusted with icing sugar. Apply the template to the sugar paste, cut around the scalloped edge and ensure the plaque is not sticking to the surface. Use a pin or a scribing tool to prick out and mark the design. Care must be taken not to mark the fresh sugar paste by leaning on the surface of the plaque.

2 Remove the paper template and, using a knitting needle or the pointed end of a paint brush handle, mark the round holes of the design by pressing right through the sugar paste. Hold the needle or paint brush at 45° to mark the oval holes and straight to mark the round holes.

3 Using a greaseproof-paper piping bag fitted with a No 0 piping tube and half-filled with royal icing, pipe around the round and oval holes with fine threads of icing. The edge may be piped in a zig-zag stitch, button-hole edging or *petit point*. Fill in the remaining design with fine lines and dots. Leave the plaque in a warm place to dry, then carefully slide the plaque on to the cake. Finish the design with fine piping around the edge of the plaque and decorate the cake with ribbons.

Broderie Anglaise Cake
A very delicate design making this cake appropriate for a christening or an anniversary cake. The broderie anglaise plaque is marked out and piped before applying it to the cake. The centre design is transferred to the sides of the cake and piped in contrasting pink royal icing on the white cake. The design is also piped on top of the cake. The petal-shaped cake is a 25 cm (10 in) light fruit cake covered with marzipan and sugar paste.

MODELLING

Marzipan and sugar paste, being pliable mediums, can be moulded like plasticine into many shapes, for example copying still-life shapes of fruit, vegetables, flowers, animals and pictures. This is great fun and is best done working with a real model in front of you so the colour and details can be copied accurately.

Colour each piece of marzipan or sugar paste to the shade you require, and simply mould each piece into the shape needed. However, always use white marzipan if adding colourings. Details may be marked in many different ways to obtain a realistic effect.

MODELLING FRUIT

Bananas: colour the marzipan or sugar paste yellow with a touch of brown and make a sausage shape with slightly tapered ends. Bend slightly to curve it along the length, then shape the ridges of the banana with a knife. Paint on the details using a fine paint brush and brown food colouring.

Grapes: colour the marzipan or sugar paste a pale-green or burgundy colour and use it to mould tiny beads. Assemble these beads into a triangular shape, then build up the layers into a bunch of grapes.

Green and black grapes

Apples: colour the marzipan or sugar paste pale green and roll it into round balls. Make an indentation at the top and bottom of each, using the end of a paint brush. Cut some cloves across in half and use the tops for the stalks and the bases as the calyces. Use red food colouring to paint the red markings.

Pears: colour the marzipan or sugar paste yellowy green and shape it into balls. Gently shape them into cones or pear shapes with the fingers. Make an indentation in the top of each with the end of a paint brush. Cut some cloves across in half and use the tops for the stalks and the bases as the calyces. Paint the pears with brown or red food colouring for the markings.

Apples and pears

Lemons: using yellow marzipan or yellow-coloured sugar paste, mould it into round balls, then roll them into oval shapes with pointed ends. Mark the skin by rolling the shapes on a fine grater. Press a clove end into each for the calyx.

Oranges: colour the marzipan or sugar paste orange and shape it into balls. Mark the skin by rolling the orange shapes on a fine grater. Mark a star shape on each with the back of a knife, and insert a clove end.

Satsumas: colour the marzipan or sugar paste a deeper orange and repeat as for making the orange, but making the shapes smaller.

Oranges and satsumas

Peaches: colour the marzipan or sugar paste a pale-peach and shape it into small balls with indentations at the tops. Mark the line around each with the back of a knife. Using pink petal dust and a dusting brush, apply the colour for the peach bloom.

Apricots: colour the marzipan or sugar paste an apricot shade and shape it into small balls. Mark the line on each with the back of a knife and make a slight indentation on the top. Using a dusting brush, dust a little pink petal dust on the surface.

Plums: colour the marzipan or sugar paste a burgundy colour and shape as for the apricot but making the shape slightly oval. Mark the line with a knife, and press a clove in the top of each for the stem.

Peaches, apricots and plums

HAND-MODELLING ANIMALS AND FIGURES

Hand-modelling is great fun, and the use of marzipan and sugar paste enables you to create individual characters with a variety of expressions and with their own individual characteristics. Look through books and greetings cards for inspiration for character shapes, or simply mould your own characters from memory.

If using marzipan, it is important to use the white variety for modelling, although the homemade variety has a wonderful flavour and the consistency is softer because of the high percentage of oil in the almonds. Always use fresh, pliable marzipan or sugar paste and do not knead in any crusted bits, as this causes the rest of the paste to become lumpy and difficult to mould.

Break down the marzipan or sugar paste into the number of pieces you require and colour them accordingly, kneading them well until evenly coloured and smooth. It is wise to use dust or paste colours as this does not affect the consistency of the marzipan, and bright vibrant colours may be obtained.

Always work with clean utensils, hands and work surface. Also wash your hands frequently as they will become sticky. Also dry them well, otherwise the paste will become tacky.

Dust the work surface and hands well with icing (confectioners') sugar. Never use cornflour (cornstarch) as this encourages mould growth, cracking and patches in the coloured paste.

Mould the figures or animals piece by piece, then assemble them and mark in any details using tools or food colouring pens.

Dry the figures off in a warm dry place, away from direct sunlight as this can fade the colours. Store them in a cardboard cake box in a dry warm place until required.

Modelling Christmas Pieces

1 Christmas trees: mould pieces of green marzipan into cone shapes and, using a pair of scissors, snip the marzipan from the point of the cone working around the cone to the base.

2 Father Christmas: cut out and shape from red sugar paste or marzipan a body, a hat, two sleeves and a red nose. Cut out and shape from white sugar paste the edging to go around the base of the body, the hat and the sleeves. Cut out the beard shape and cover with white sugar paste pressed through a sieve; also use this for his hair. Colour some sugar paste to a flesh tone and shape the head and hands. Assemble the parts together using a little egg white or gum glaze to secure. Mark in the eyes with a food colouring pen.

3 Reindeer: using brown-coloured marzipan, shape an oblong body piece and make a cut at each end to within 1 cm (½ in) of the centre. Shape the hoofs and bend to form front and back legs. Mould a heart-shaped piece for the head, press the top curves into antlers and snip with a pair of scissors to shape. Place in position on the body, attach the ears and make a red nose. Use a brown food colouring pen for the markings.

4 Sack with presents: shape a piece of brown marzipan into a ball. Using a modelling tool, press the inside to make it hollow, making the edge thinner. Shape presents from red and green sugar paste or marzipan.

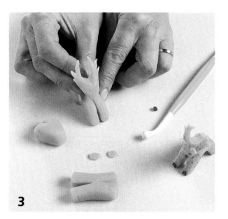

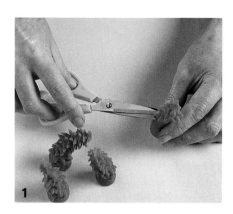

Christmas Cake
It is always fun at Christmas to have novelty figures on a cake rather than shop-bought items. The hand-modelled Father Christmas, sack, presents, trees and reindeer are made from marzipan. The cake is a 20 cm (8 in) square rich fruit cake covered in marzipan, with a flat top and peaked royal-icing sides. Arrange the figures on top of the cake and to finish trim the board with ribbon.

Modelling Circus Figures

1 Elephant: using dark-grey sugar paste, shape an oblong body, make a cross cut and shape into a body with four legs. Shape a cone for the head and elongate the thin end into a trunk. Shape two grey ears. Roll out small beads of sugar paste to make two eyes and two thin tusks and for the detail on the feet. Assemble the pieces together with egg white or gum glaze. Shape the pink hat and red ribbon from sugar paste, and then assemble and fit together.

2 Seal: mould black sugar paste into a cone shape; start at the head end and shape to a point and shape the remaining body and tail. Mould the balls from coloured sugar paste.

3 Clown: place strips of red and black sugar paste on to a rolled out piece of white sugar paste. Roll lightly to give a striped effect. Shape an oblong piece of white sugar paste, then cover with a strip of striped sugar paste. Make a cut half-way through to form the body and legs of the clown. Line the inside of the legs with more striped sugar paste. Shape the arms and ball in the same way. Mould and cut out the remaining pieces – red and black frills for the hat, ruffs for the neck, sleeves and legs. Shape a red mouth, nose and a cone for the hat, two black shoes, a flesh-coloured head and hands and a white mask shape. Use brown sugar paste pressed through a sieve for the hair. Assemble all the pieces and secure with egg white or gum glaze.

4 Bucket of foam: use two rounds of green and one round of black sugar paste. Press them together and hollow out the centre with a modelling tool. Make a handle from a piece of black and green sugar paste. Press some cream-coloured sugar paste through a sieve and fill up the bucket. Shape the handle and press in position.

1

4

2

3

Circus Cake

A fun cake for any age, with hand-modelled clown, seals, elephant, bucket and balls, this 20 cm (8 in) round Madeira cake is covered with marzipan and the top of the cake with white sugar paste. The strip of white sugar paste for the side has thin lengths of red and black sugar paste positioned diagonally across it. When the sugar paste is rolled thinly, the red and black sugar paste blends into the white. Knead the trimmings together and make a thin roll to fit around the top of the cake and crimp it in position. Finally arrange the circus figures on top of the cake.

PIPING TECHNIQUES

The art of piping is regarded by many as both mysterious and difficult. However, this is not necessarily the case, and piping is a skill well worth mastering. The key to success is to practise at every opportunity, and to have infinite patience. All that is needed for this technique is a good-quality piping bag or a greaseproof-paper piping bag fitted with a straight-sided metal tube. With these items of equipment, cream, butter icing and royal icing may be transformed into stars, shells, flowers, scrolls and lines to create simple yet highly effective decorations on a cake that will be admired by all who see them.

SIMPLE PIPING TECHNIQUES

Although it appears complicated and difficult to do, with practice and following the few guidelines below, it is amazing how quickly you will become confident in using a piping bag and tube. Take every opportunity you can to pipe creams, meringue, butter icing and royal icing instead of just spreading or swirling them. Try out simple designs at first, to get the feel of using and controlling a piping bag and tube. When you feel confident, try more advanced designs but keeping to just a few differently shaped tubes. Introduce colour to a cake with a contrasting shade of piped icing, or pipe white icing on a coloured base cake. Only as the skill with which you handle the piping bag, tube and icing increases will you be ready to add to the range of tubes you use.

PIPING EQUIPMENT

Commercially made piping bags: these are available ready-made in washable fabric from most cake specialists or kitchen shops. As they are easy to handle, they are especially good for beginners. Sizes vary from small to large and they are ideal for piping cream, butter icing and meringue icing.

Paper piping bags: the great advantage of a greaseproof-paper piping bag is that it can be made in advance in various sizes and may be used with or without an icing tube. If used without a tube, simply fill the bag with icing, fold down the top and snip off the end to pipe lines, or cut a 'V'-shape to pipe leaves. After use they are simply thrown away. If the icing runs out, simply fill a new bag or transfer the icing tube to a new greaseproof-paper piping bag. Choose a good-quality greaseproof or baking parchment for making the bags and then follow the instructions on page 104.

Icing tubes: these are available in such a wide variety of shapes and sizes it is quite difficult to know which ones to choose. As a beginner, it is advisable to start with a small selection of straight-sided metal icing tubes as they give clean, sharp results. Choose two writing tubes and small, medium and large star tubes to start. After mastering the use of these, build up your collection as you try new piping designs. Keep them clean and store them carefully in a box or rigid container so they do not get damaged. Always clean icing tubes with a special cleaning brush so that the ends do not become bent or damaged.

To Make a Greaseproof-Paper Piping Bag

1 Cut out a 38 × 25 cm (15 × 10 in) rectangle of greaseproof paper or baking parchment. Fold this in half diagonally and cut along the fold line to form two triangular shapes, each with a blunt end.

Fold the blunt end of the triangle over into the centre to make a sharp cone and hold it in position.

2 Then fold the sharp end of the triangle over the cone shape. Hold all the points together at the back of the cone, ensuring the point of the cone is sharp.

3 Turn the points inside the top edge of the cone and crease firmly. Secure with sticky tape or staple if wished.

1

2

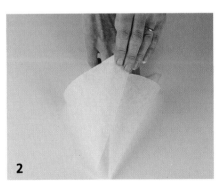

3

ICING CONSISTENCIES

Before using any piping equipment, it is essential to have a butter icing, icing or cream of the correct consistency. If using icing or butter icing, when a wooden spoon is drawn out of the icing it should form a fine but sharp point. If the icing is too stiff it will be very difficult to squeeze out of the bag; if too soft the icing will be difficult to control and the piped shapes will rapidly lose their definition.

When piping dairy cream, the consistency needs to be much softer. Whip the cream until it peaks softly (over-whipping causes curdling and unsightly piping). Once the cream is in the piping bag it may feel too soft, but the warmth of the hands causes the cream to thicken and sometimes even curdle. For this reason, only half-fill the piping bag with dairy cream as it will then be less of a waste if this happens.

Piping consistency for butter icing

Piping consistency for royal icing

Piping consistency for dairy cream

BASIC PIPING

When piping any cake with butter icing, royal icing or dairy cream, it is best to practise piping on a board or work surface before starting on the cake. Also ensure the icing is the correct colour and consistency.

Use a greaseproof-paper or a nylon piping bag fitted with a straight-sided metal tube as this gives a clean sharp defined pattern when piping.

Half-fill the bag with icing – do not be tempted to fill it to the top as the more full the icing bag is, the harder it is to squeeze the icing out of the tube. This results in aching wrists and hands and poor piping. A good guide to follow is the smaller the icing tube, the less icing you require.

To pipe royal icing or butter icing: hold the piping bag comfortably with the tube through the first two fingers and thumb, like holding a pencil. Apply the pressure at the top of the bag. The wrists and arms should be relaxed, just ready to guide the tube.

To pipe dairy cream: it is better to use a nylon piping bag fitted with a larger tube to pipe whipped cream into swirls, shells or stars. Half-fill the bag with whipped cream and twist the top of the bag so the cream comes to the end of the tube. Holding the top of the bag with one hand and the tube with the other, gently press out the cream into the desired shape, twisting the bag as it empties.

SIMPLE PIPED SHAPES

Piping is the obvious choice when decorating a cake, but beginners are easily discouraged by complicated piping designs. Choose a simple star icing tube and fit it into a greaseproof-paper piping bag to pipe swirls, scrolls and shells.

To pipe a swirl: half-fill the greaseproof-paper piping bag fitted with a star tube. Fold down the top and squeeze the icing to the end of the tube. Place the icing tube on the surface of the cake, press out the icing and pipe a swirl of icing in a circular movement. Stop pressing the bag and pull up sharply to break the icing. Repeat to pipe swirls around the top edge and base of the cake, if desired.

To pipe a star: pipe a star shape using a star tube, as before, holding the bag straight above the surface of the cake. Press the icing out, forming a star on the edge of the cake, then pull off to break the icing. Repeat all around the cake to make a neat border.

To pipe scrolls: hold the piping bag at an angle so that the icing tube is almost on its side in front of you. Press out the icing on to the top edge of the cake to secure the scroll. Pipe outwards in a circular movement and return the icing tube to the edge of the cake. Stop pressing the bag and break off the icing. Repeat again, but pipe the icing away from the edge of the cake in a circular movement, then return the icing tube just to the edge. This is called a reverse scroll, piping a scroll inwards and then one outwards. For a straight scroll design, pipe the scrolls in one direction only.

To pipe shells: hold the piping bag at an angle to the cake so that the icing tube is almost on its side in front of you. Press out some icing and secure it to the surface of the cake, pressing gently. Move the icing tube forward, then move it slowly up, over and down in what is almost a rocking movement. Stop pressing and break off the

Piping a border of stars with dairy cream

Piping a reverse-scroll border with crème au beurre

Piping a shell border with royal icing

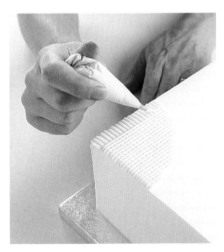

Piping a trellis design with royal icing

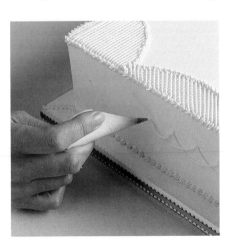

Piping dropped-loop thread work

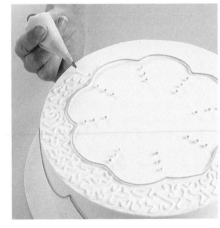

Piping a filigree or cornelli design

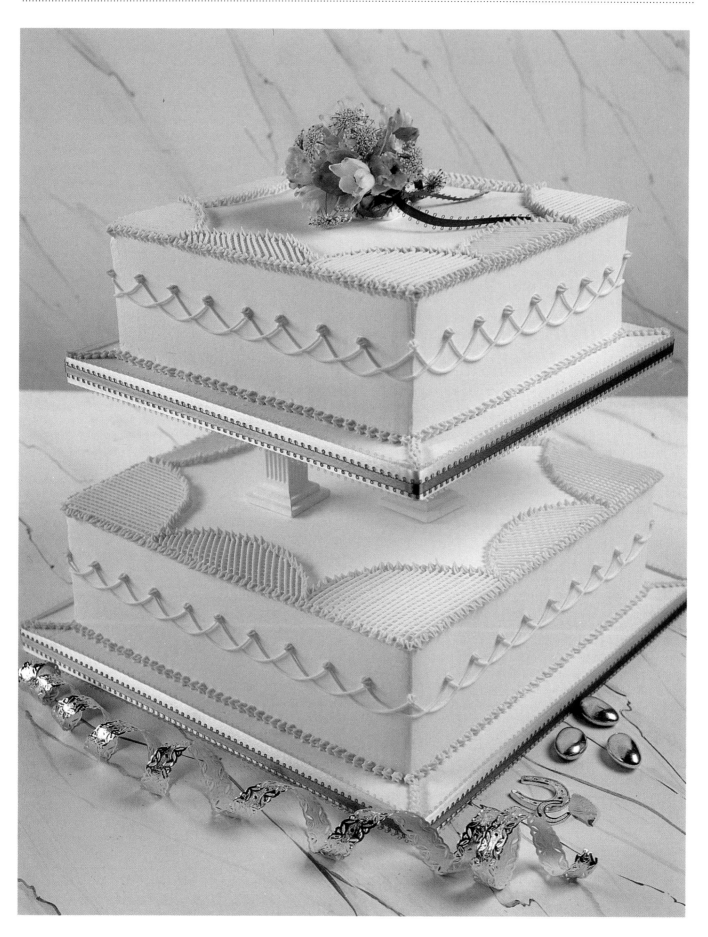

icing by pulling the tube towards you. Repeat this process, piping the icing on to the end of the first shell to give a shell edging.

To pipe lines: fit the piping bag with a plain writing tube (the smaller the hole the finer the lines) and half-fill it with icing. Pipe a thread of icing, securing the end to the surface of the cake. Continue to pipe the icing just above the surface of the cake, allowing the thread to fall in a straight or curved line. When the line is finished stop pressing and break off the icing.

To pipe a trellis design: pipe parallel lines of icing in one direction, then over-pipe the lines in the opposite direction. A third line may be piped across the lattice-work to give an even better finish. The lines may be piped diagonally or straight, depending on the finished result required.

Dropped-loop thread work: using a plain writing tube, pipe a thread of icing, securing the end to the side of the cake. Continue to pipe the icing just away from the side of the cake so the thread forms a loop. Stop pressing when the loop is long enough, join the icing loop on to the side of the cake and break it off. Repeat piping more loops. Once the loops have been piped all around the cake, it is possible to repeat the procedure to over-pipe each loop making them double width,

---

Trellis Wedding Cake
A two-tiered cake consisting of a 20 cm (8 in) and a 25 cm (10 in) square rich fruit cake, each covered with marzipan and flat royal icing. The trellis design is based on a square template with a scalloped edge. The ends of the trellis design are piped with tiny stars to neaten the edges. The side design has been marked at 2.5 cm (1 in) intervals and piped with dropped loop thread work. White and blue ribbons trim the cake boards, and a fresh flower arrangement decorates the top.

or dropping slightly to make longer loops. There are endless designs possible with this dropped-loop thread work which looks particularly attractive on the side of a cake.

To pipe leaves: half-fill an uncut greaseproof-paper piping bag with icing and press the icing to the end of the bag. Cut the end of the piping bag into an inverted 'V'-shape. Place the tip on the surface of the cake and press out the icing to form a leaf shape, then sharply break off the icing. Repeat to make a pretty border, or just to decorate flowers or to make a design.

Filigree or cornelli work: half-fill a greaseproof-paper piping bag, fitted with a plain writing tube, with icing. Holding the piping bag like a pen between the thumb and forefinger, pipe threads of icing into 'W'- and 'M'-shapes, keeping the flow of the icing constant. Remember to work in all directions, not in lines.

To pipe beads or dots: piping beads of icing is quite simple, but the icing has to be of a softer consistency so there is not a sharp point on the end of the bead which has been piped. Trial and error will produce icing of the correct consistency.

Fit a greaseproof-paper piping bag with a size No 3 plain tube, half-fill with icing and fold down the top. Press the icing out just above the surface of the cake to form a rounded bulb of icing, then pull upwards sharply to break off the icing. Repeat to make a border of nicely rounded beads of icing.

To Pipe a Basket-Weave Design

1 Fit one greaseproof-paper piping bag with a ribbon tube and another piping bag with a medium-sized plain writing tube. Pipe a vertical line from the top of the cake to the bottom with the plain writing tube. Then carefully pipe 2 cm (¾ in) lines across the vertical line at 1.5 cm (½ in) intervals with the ribbon tube.

2 Pipe another vertical line of icing on the edge of the horizontal lines with the plain tube again. Repeat to pipe more 2 cm (¾ in) lines of icing with the ribbon tube across the vertical line and in between the spaces to form a basket-weave. Repeat all around the cake.

3 The basket-weave design can then be continued over the top of the cake in the same way.

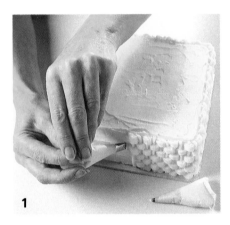

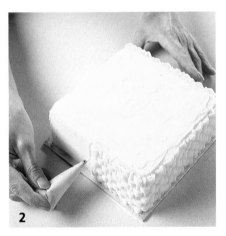

Basket-Weave Cake
This butter-iced wedding cake is made of two square Madeira cakes, one 23 cm (9 in) and one 15 cm (6 in). The surfaces of the cakes are completely covered with basket-weave piping. The layers are left to set, then placed together, one on top of the other. Choose any fresh flowers to be positioned at the last minute – these fuchsias provide a particularly stunning flash of colour.

SIMPLE PIPED FLOWERS

With the use of a petal tube, many simple flowers can be piped. The sizes of the tubes used are small, medium and large, and can be purchased for both right- and left-handers. Fit the tube in a greaseproof-paper piping bag, half-fill this with royal icing and fold down the top. Practise several times to get the feel of the nozzle. It is also easier to pipe on to a flower nail or piping turntable.

Rose: secure a piece of waxed paper to the piping turntable with a bead of icing. On the paper, pipe the cone-shaped centre using a petal tube, turning the turntable at the same time. Make sure you keep the piping tube upright and the wide side of the tube towards the base.

Pipe a petal two-thirds of the way round the centre cone, turning the turntable at the same time. Repeat to pipe another three petals, rotating the turntable and keeping the top of each petal curled outwards.

Hold the piping bag at an angle (instead of upright) to pipe the final petals of the rose almost flat. This will give the finished rose the look of being in full bloom.

Rosebud: this is just a simpler and smaller version of the rose. Pipe the centre cone and then three petals close together following the technique described above.

Daisy: using the icing turntable covered with a square of waxed paper secured with a bead of icing, hold the petal tube on its side so it is flat. Pipe a tiny petal shape in a flat loop, at the same time turning the turntable. Continue to pipe about 12 tiny petals in a circle. Using yellow icing, pipe small beads to fill the centre.

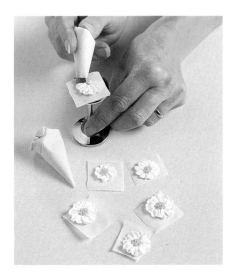

Pansy: pipe the pansy petals like those of the daisy, using white, yellow or purple icing. Holding the petal tube flat, pipe the petal shape in a large rounded loop while turning the turntable. Pipe another two petals, one on each side, with the wide side of the tube to the centre. Pipe the fourth petal on the left-hand side of the third petal. Then pipe the last petal from the centre of the fourth petal and pipe all the way round to form a circle.

Pipe yellow threads of icing in the centre. Using food colouring pens, colour in the markings of the pansy.

Forget-me-not: have ready white and pale-blue royal icing. Half-fill the piping bag with white on the wide side of the tube, and the blue on the narrow side. Fold down the top and press the icing to the end of the tube.

Hold the petal tube almost flat with the wide side of the tube to the centre and pipe a rounded petal, at the same time revolving the turntable. Pipe another four petals, each overlapping the first, to form a circle. Pipe a bead of yellow icing in the centre.

Apple blossom: pipe these as for the forget-me-not, but using pale-pink and white icing, and finish with piped green dots in the centre.

Piped Flower Cake

A pretty cake suitable for almost any occasion, be it a birthday, Mother's Day, Easter, anniversary or even a christening. The cake is a 20 cm (8 in) round rich fruit cake covered with marzipan and sugar paste. The edge of the cake has been crimped using a scalloped crimper and the edge trimmed with ribbon. The floral design is made up of piped roses, daisies, apple blossoms, forget-me-nots, pansies and narcissi.

Primrose: use pale-yellow icing and hold the petal tube almost flat with the wide side of the tube to the centre and start piping a petal. Revolve the turntable as you go. Half-way round each petal move the tube in towards the centre and out again, making a small 'V'-shape in the centre of each petal. Pipe five petals, each overlapping, and the last petal on the top. When the flowers are dry, paint the centre with blossom tints in a deeper yellow colour.

Narcissus: pipe white petals as for the forget-me-not, but move the tube out and in again to form a long-shaped petal. Pipe the first three petals apart, then pipe the remaining three petals in between these. Pipe a coil of yellow icing from a No 1 plain writing tube to form the centre. Paint the top with orange food colouring for a different variety of narcissus.

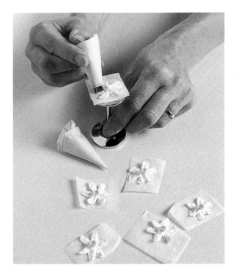

ADVANCED PIPING

The following techniques will require a little more time and patience to master, but with practice you will soon achieve very pleasing results.

LACE-WORK

Piped lace-work is a very delicate way of decorating a wedding cake and seems a natural choice as wedding dresses and veils are often made of or feature very fine lace-work.

Although the pieces are very fragile, when properly made it is quite easy to transfer the pieces to the cake and transport them without breakage. Small pieces of lace-work are used as an edging or a border, or as a contrast to frills and flounces and extension work. Large pieces may be used to replace flounces around the base of a cake and to add a delicate finish to a simply iced cake.

Designing lace pieces is quite easy, using lace patterns from a book or copying a lace ribbon edging or lace inserts from a dress.

Ensure the royal icing is of the correct consistency and that double-strength egg albumen has been used (no glycerine should be added to egg-white royal icing). Quarter-fill a greaseproof-paper piping bag fitted with a No 0 plain writing tube and fold down the top. As only a small amount of icing is used to pipe these fine pieces, this will ensure that the bag may be held comfortably like a pen and prevent the wrists and hands from aching.

To Make Lace Pieces

1 Once you have chosen or designed the shape you require, draw the design boldly on a piece of paper. Repeat the design several times, so that once you start piping you can continue. Place the design on a flat surface and cover it with a piece of run-out film, waxed paper or baking parchment. Secure the edges with tape or beads of icing.

2 Most lace-work consists of small curves and lines, so the tube is used very close to the surface and even pressure should be applied while piping. Uneven pressure will cause uneven lines and too little pressure will produce weak spots which will easily break.

3 It is also important that all the lines of lace must touch as any gap causes a weakness and the pieces may then break. It is sensible to pipe more pieces than required to allow for breakages. Allow the pieces to dry flat in a warm place, then carefully run a fine palette knife underneath the lace to release each piece.

4 Apply the pieces of lace-work to the cake with beads of royal icing. If the lace pieces need to be stored, leave them on the run-out film or waxed paper and store in a cardboard box in a warm dry place.

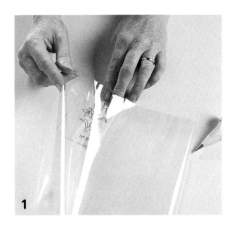

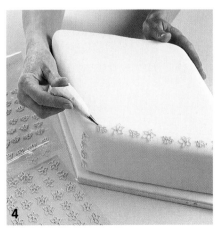

TUBE EMBROIDERY

Embroidery is made up of many different colours and shades of icing, piped in the traditional embroidery stitch shapes to build up a pattern, floral design or picture.

Before embarking on any embroidery design, it is essential first to practise each of the embroidery stitches, which are made up of tiny loops, curved lines, dots and crosses. Once these basic stitches have been mastered, make up simple designs to go on to a plaque and see how effective it can be.

Designs may be inspired by embroidery paper patterns, fabric and wallpaper designs, porcelain and china patterns or old, embroidered table linen. Once the design has been established, trace or draw it as accurately as possible on greaseproof paper, then transfer the design on to the sugar plaque or sugar-pasted cake using a pin. Mark only the main outline of the design as too much detail will be confusing when you come to pipe it.

Once the colour scheme has been worked out, divide the royal icing into the number of colours or shades required. Tint or colour the icing according to the pattern, making sure it is soft enough to flow easily, and place a small amount of each colour into a greaseproof-paper piping bag fitted with a No 0 plain writing tube. Small quantities in the bag are comfortable to hold and allow more freedom of movement for piping close to the surface in order to obtain an accurate design.

Start piping with the tube gently scraping the surface as the icing is pressed out, using an even pressure and holding the piping bag like a pen. Pipe the background of the design and work towards the front. Complete one section at a time, changing the shades where necessary. Pipe lighter colours over darker shades, while still wet, before moving on to the next part of the design. This way you produce a smooth result and the shades will blend well. However, if the stitches appear rather uneven or little tails are showing, draw a fine damp paint brush through the stitches to flatten them slightly.

To Make an Embroidery Design

1 Using a paper embroidery pattern or a traced design of your own, place it over the sugar plaque and carefully mark out the design using a marker or stainless steel pin.

2 Using two shades of green royal icing, place it into greaseproof-paper piping bags fitted with No 1 plain writing tubes. Pipe stem stitch to fill in the stems and fishbone stitch to fill in the leaves, blending the colours to give a realistic effect.

3 Using two shades of pink and No 1 plain writing tubes, fill in the petals using long and short stitch. Pipe the long stitch in the deeper shade, and the short stitch using the lighter coloured icing.

4 Work the side design using white royal icing and a No 1 plain writing tube. Pipe single chain stitch for the outline of the flowers and leaves. Pipe French knots of icing to form the bunches of grapes and buds, and fine lines for the stems. Infill the design with pink and green icing using satin stitch, long and short stitch and French knots.

EMBROIDERY STITCHES

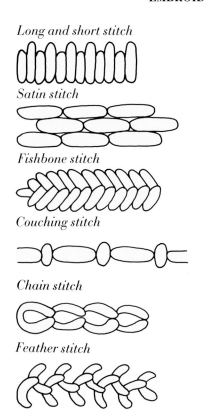

Long and short stitch

Satin stitch

Fishbone stitch

Couching stitch

Chain stitch

Feather stitch

Herringbone stitch

Fern stitch

Star stitch

Stem stitch

Cross stitch

French knots

1

Embroidered Cake
A delicate cake which would make a birthday, christening, Mother's Day or anniversary celebration complete.

The design has been applied to a sugar paste plaque so that it may be kept as a keepsake, while the side design has been marked out and then

piped directly on to the cake. A 20 cm (8 in) oval light fruit cake has been covered with marzipan and soft-pink sugar paste.

EXTENSION WORK

This is a method of decorating the sides of a cake by piping fine lines of icing in a horizontal series of dropped loops piped exactly on top of the previous loops to form a solid bridge. Vertical lines of icing are then piped from a marked design on the side of the cake down to the base of the bridge. The piping must be extremely neat, straight and accurate, so an enormous amount of patience and time is required.

The extension work should always be designed carefully and accurately to complement the shape of the cake and any other decorations included in the design. Other decorations that will complement this beautiful technique are lace pieces, tube embroidery, flowers and ribbon insertion.

When piping extension work, the cake base must have straight sides and a coating of smooth sugar paste or icing free from any blemishes or major faults, as this work will not hide any flaws in the icing.

The icing being piped must be well made, soft, smooth and of a good texture. It must also be free of any lumps which may block the piping tube. The addition of liquid glucose will give the icing a greater elasticity, which is a great advantage when piping vertical lines. Use 1 ml ($\frac{1}{4}$ tsp) of liquid glucose to each egg white and leave the egg white for 24 hours at room temperature before use. Ensure the icing sugar is sifted through a very fine sieve to eliminate any lumps which could cause the tube to block and the threads of icing to break.

Make an icing of medium-peak consistency and ensure it has been beaten well and is light in texture so that it will flow easily through the piping tube. Decide on the design of the extension work and make the template accordingly.

To make the template: cut a strip of greaseproof paper the length and depth of the side of the cake, fold the strip in half as many times as required to make the paper template the width

of the scallop required. Draw a semicircle at the base of the template and cut out. The width of the base scallop is usually about 2.5 cm (1 in). Now cut the top edge of the template to the shape and depth required for the vertical lines.

Method

1 Secure the template around the side of the cake with sticky tape and, using a pin, mark the top edge of the design and the scalloped shape at the base.

Place the cake on a turntable, if using, so that it is at eye level and tilt it away from you. Using a pin, re-mark the high points of the scallop design so that you are in no doubt where the loops start and finish.

2 To work the bridge, touch the cake with the tube at the highest point of the scallop and press out a little icing to attach the thread. Pull the tube just away from the cake and maintain an even pressure of icing to pipe the thread, allowing it to follow the scallop line. Touch the scallop at the next highest point on the design. Continue piping and work around the cake, making sure the first row of bridge work is dry before starting on the second. There should be no gaps between the cake and scallops as this can cause a weak bridge.

3 Pipe each loop exactly over the preceding loop, finishing the thread just slightly shorter on each. Pipe about six loops to build up the bridge, then allow the piping to dry before piping the extension work.

4 To pipe the extension work, tilt the cake towards you so that the lines fall straight. Touch the cake with the tube at the top of the design to attach the thread of icing and pull away immediately, taking care not to form a bulb of icing at the top. Pipe vertical lines just beyond the bridge, then remove the ends with a fine damp paint brush. The lines should be parallel and so close together that you cannot pipe a line in between them.

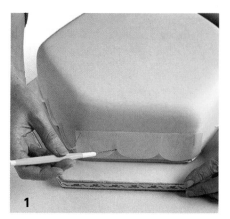

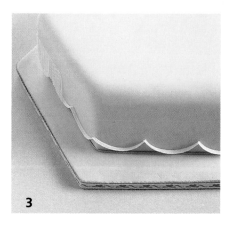

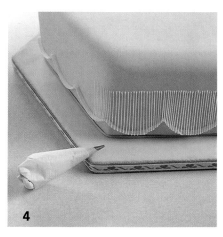

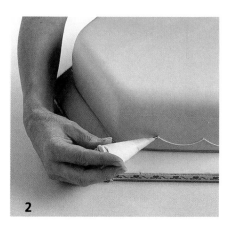

Hexagonal Wedding Cake
A beautiful centrepiece for any wedding, this cake is decorated with scalloped extension work and piped embroidery. The arrangement of white freesia with pink ribbons is just enough to enhance this cake. The cake is a 30 cm (12 in) hexagonal rich fruit cake covered with marzipan and soft-pink sugar paste. The colour and floral decoration may be changed to suit the occasion.

LETTERING

Lettering or writing on a cake can often be daunting for most people, simply because they are worried about making a mistake on a finished cake or because they have not developed a distinctive style of writing. When you start writing you will have no particular style, although with some practice you will soon develop one which is suited to your own hand. It is very disappointing when you try to pipe free-hand writing and you find it is either too cramped, too spaced-out, sloping upwards or downhill and generally looking unattractive.

Firstly, look at lettering samples in cake books and copy a style you like. Study it in depth, then draw it on a piece of paper and cover it with a piece of perspex (plexiglass). Using a No 1 plain writing tube and royal icing, pipe the letters over and over again in the chosen style. You can practise writing the style on a pad while doodling on the telephone, or even use it to write a letter so that it becomes second nature to write free-hand in the chosen style.

Keep practising on the perspex and wiping it clean. Pipe 'Happy Birthday', 'Congratulations', 'Good Luck', for example. Always calculate beforehand the number of letters in each word and learn how much space the letters take up so that you can space them evenly apart on the surface of the cake. If you still feel unsure about the spacing of the letters, it would be sensible to trace them on a piece of greaseproof paper and mark the letters on the cake with a pin. Pipe the letters in white royal icing first, and then re-pipe in coloured icing to finish the shapes.

Lettering may also be produced in the form of run-outs (see pages 117–120). There are many styles to choose from, such as basic shaped letters or Gothic script. All these run-out letters may be coloured, left plain, or have additional piping when they are completely dry. Floral lettering with piped flowers on each letter, dotted lettering and monograms also offer different techniques and finishes.

Angela Cake
This 25 cm (10 in) light fruit cake covered with marzipan and royal icing is ideal for an 18th or 21st birthday cake. It is decorated with a simple scallop design, both on the top and side, piped using a No 1 plain writing tube. Pipe the design in white icing first, then over-pipe in the colour required. The design is finished with cornelli work in white royal icing and lettering.

If unsure of your lettering skills, start with names and greetings formed of carefully spaced capital letters. Pipe the letters in white royal icing first, then over-pipe in coloured icing.

With practice, you will develop an attractive free-hand writing style.

Letters and numbers in the form of run-outs are an alternative decoration to free-hand lettering. See pages 117–120 for instructions.

ICING RUN-OUTS

Icing run-outs are one of the most exacting forms of cake decoration. They can be made in any shape or form by simply tracing over a chosen design or pattern.

Once made, small run-outs keep well placed between layers of waxed paper in a box stored in a dry place. So if a large quantity of run-outs are needed to decorate a cake, they can be made in advance. Larger run-outs and collars (see overleaf) are more difficult to keep as they may warp during storage. These should be made, allowed to dry completely and then applied to the cake.

Run-outs are made from royal icing and are very fragile, so it is wise to start with a small solid shape, and make more than you need to allow for breakages. When you are confident at making the simple small solid shapes, practise making finer pieces, figures and scenes. Accuracy, not speed, is important when making run-outs, so always allow plenty of time.

ROYAL ICING CONSISTENCIES

The consistency and texture of the icing must be right or the run-outs will be difficult to make and handle. Use double-strength dried-egg albumen or egg whites, with no additives such as glycerine or lemon juice. The icing should be light and glossy, not heavy and dull. When the spoon is lifted, a soft peak should form which bends over at the tip. This is the consistency required for piping the outline of the run-outs.

Icing to fill in the run-out must be soft enough to flow with the help of a paint brush, but just holding its shape until tapped, then becoming smooth. Dilute the royal icing with reconstituted double-strength egg albumen and test a little on a flat surface to test the consistency. If possible leave the icing to stand overnight, covered with damp muslin (cheesecloth), to allow any air bubbles to come to the surface. Then stir the icing until it is completely smooth.

MAKING AN ICING RUN-OUT

Draw or trace the chosen design several times on a piece of paper, well spaced apart. Place the paper on a flat surface and cover with a piece of perspex (plexiglass) or glass. Cover the design with a piece of run-out film or waxed paper and secure to the perspex or glass with tape or icing.

Fit a greaseproof-paper piping bag with a No 0 or 1 writing tube and half-fill with icing to pipe the outline. Fill several greaseproof-paper piping bags with soft icing, fold down the tops and leave to one side.

Pipe carefully around the outline of the design with a continuous thread of icing or with as few breaks as possible. To do this, squeeze out a little icing at the least obvious point of the run-out and secure the icing thread to the film or paper. Lift the thread of icing just above the surface and squeeze the bag gently, allowing the thread to fall on the line marking the run-out shape. Join the icing where it started.

Snip the pointed end off one soft icing bag and fill in the run-out. Start by piping around the inside edge to keep the outline soft, otherwise it may break. Then work towards the centre, filling the shape so that the icing looks rounded and over-filled – the icing will shrink as it sets.

Use a fine paint brush or cocktail stick (toothpick) to ensure the area is completely filled, and the icing is smooth and rounded. Gently tap the board so that any bubbles rise to the surface. If they do, burst them with a pin. If the run-out is large, leave it in position and lift off the perspex (plexiglass) or glass with the run-out in place on it and leave to dry. For small run-outs, carefully release the film or waxed paper and transfer the run-out to a flat board to dry. Replace the perspex or glass and cover the design with more run-out film or waxed paper and repeat to make as many run-outs as required. If possible, leave the run-outs under a spotlight to dry the surface quickly; otherwise leave them in a warm dry place overnight. The more quickly they are dried, the glossier they will be. Carefully peel off the paper from the run-outs and decorate the cake, securing them in place with small beads or a line of royal icing. Otherwise, leave the run-outs on the paper and store them in a box between layers of waxed paper.

Run-Out Corner Pieces

1 Place the run-out film over the chosen pencilled design. Pipe the outline of the corner pieces using a No 0 plain writing tube and white royal icing.

2 Half-fill several greaseproof-paper piping bags with yellow royal icing, snip off the points of the bags and fill in the corner pieces as quickly and as evenly as possible.

3 When the run-out pieces are completely dry, loosen them very carefully using a fine cranked-handle palette knife.

4 Turn the run-out corner pieces over and pipe fine lines of royal icing from a No 0 plain writing tube, working diagonally from edge to edge. Complete the lines in one direction, then pipe in the opposite direction to form a trellis pattern.

5 When the trellis work is dry, attach the corner pieces to the cake with royal icing.

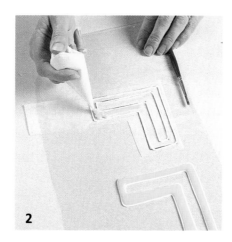

2

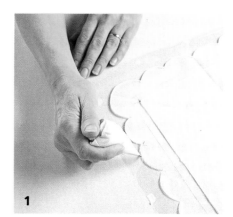

3

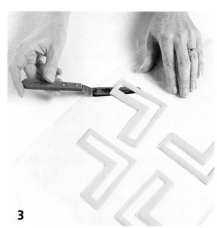

4

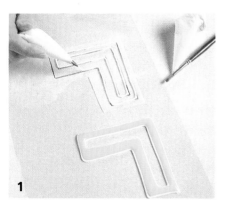

1

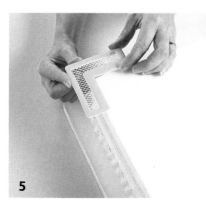

5

Run-Out Collar

1 Secure the run-out film over the chosen collar design with a few beads of royal icing. When positioned firmly pipe the outline of the collar using a No 1 plain writing tube and white royal icing.

2 Have several greaseproof-paper piping bags half-filled with yellow royal icing ready. Snip off the point of one bag and begin to fill in the collar, working as quickly and neatly as possible.

3 Use a fine paint brush to coax the yellow icing to the white icing outline, taking care not to touch it with the brush or it may break.

4 Continue to fill in the collar, working from both sides until the collar is completely filled in with yellow icing.

5 When the collar has dried completely, pipe the bead edging and embroidery design on the collar.

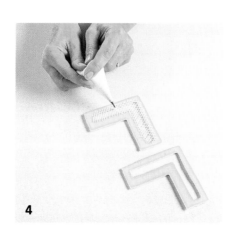

1

2

Scalloped Run-Out Cake

A cake with a formal appearance with run-out initials would suit a 21st birthday, a congratulations cake or a retirement cake. The run-out collar and initials may be made in any colour and the ribbons chosen to match. The 23 cm (9 in) square rich fruit cake is covered with marzipan and smooth royal icing which supports the collar, giving the cake a very classical appearance.

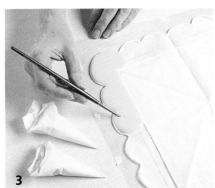

3

4

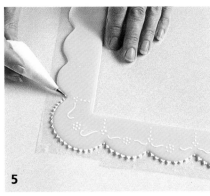

5

RUN-OUT MOTIFS

Run-out piped figures are fun to make. They may be produced on run-out film and applied directly to the cake, or made on a sugar plaque which is then placed on the cake.

These figures look very different from normal run-outs as they take on a three-dimensional appearance with individual sections filled with differently coloured icings.

They are then painted with details, using food colouring pens or a paint brush and paste colours. Small additions such as sugar-paste flowers or piped details may also be added when the run-out is dry.

To choose a suitable figure for a motif have a look at greetings cards, children's books, gift-wrapping paper, fabrics and wallpaper patterns. From these ideas you may wish to create your own special motif or copy one direct. Always keep in mind that the figure which you choose must be simple in shape and not too intricate in detail, as each section has to be completed separately.

To interpret the design of the motif, the figure must be outlined in various sections. This separates the parts of the motif to be filled in with differently coloured icings. Alternatively, these may be filled in with white icing and painted by hand when the motif is completely dry.

Once you have drawn your figure, ensure the size is correct to fit the cake you are decorating as sometimes it is necessary to enlarge or reduce the picture so that it is in keeping with the scale of the cake. The quickest and simplest way is to photocopy; any up-to-date machine will reduce or enlarge the image for you and this enables you to experiment with various sizes. Otherwise, working on graph paper, space the design over proportionately more or fewer squares and draw the figure free-hand. Another method is to use a pantograph: as you follow the outline with one end, the pencil at the other end copies the enlarged or reduced image on to a piece of paper.

Method

1 Trace the design, place it on a flat surface and cover it with a piece of perspex (plexiglass). Cover the perspex with run-out film, securing the edges with tape. Alternatively, you could transfer the design on to a sugar plaque, using a pin to mark the design or over-tracing the design with a pencil.

2 Make the run-out icing to the slightly thicker consistency and tint to the colours required (see page 48). Outlines for the run-out are not used here, so fill in the sections in stages, allowing the surface of each to skin over before filling in adjacent sections, otherwise the icings will merge and you will lose definition.

3 Pipe details, such as here, with a plain writing tube.

4 Use a fine paint brush to guide the soft icing to fill the shape required.

5 To obtain the different levels of icing in the various sections it is necessary to run some of the icing in level, then fill in other sections full and rounded to obtain the contrast. When the motif has been completely filled in, leave it to dry under a spotlight or in a warm dry place.

6 Finish the motif by adding the details, which may either be piped as here, painted or produced in the form of appliquéd sugar pieces. The motif should look bright and glossy, and include varying textures and levels of icing.

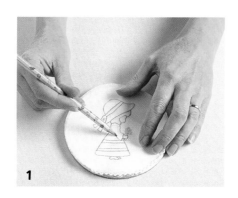

Motif Cake
Choose a design from a card, book or picture and transfer the design on to a sugar plaque. The cake will suit any occasion you require such as birthday, Mother's or Father's Day, christening or anniversaries. Make the sugar plaque from flower paste and allow it to dry before completing the design. The cake is a 20 cm (8 in) light fruit cake, covered with marzipan and royal icing. The ribbons and simple piping are coloured to match the plaque. The plaque may be kept afterwards as a memento of the occasion.

WORKING WITH FLOWER PASTE

This remarkable medium is used mostly for modelling very fine sugar flowers, sugar plaques and intricate items. When made into a paste, it is exceptionally easy to work with as it can be rolled out so thinly that you can see through it. It may be moulded or cut into flower shapes, and it dries so quickly that the flowers set in such a way that they look almost real.

Flowers made from flower paste may be wired on to stems and shaped into sprays and bouquets, and when they are dry the paste is exceptionally hard, almost like ceramic flowers. Flower paste is also wonderful for making a *pastillage* plaque (see pages 134–135): any shape or size may be made and the edges of the plaque can be frilled or crimped. When the plaque is dry, it is as hard as a ceramic tile, which makes working on the plaque exceptionally easy. Flowers may be applied to it, or piping or free-hand pictures drawn on using food colouring pens or other colourings and a fine paint brush.

Sold as 'petal paste', this may be purchased at any cake-decorating shop in 250 g (8 oz) packets or 450 g (1 lb) packets. To make up the paste, you just add water. It is, however, very expensive to buy if a large quantity is required and should therefore be used with due respect.

There is a recipe for flower paste on page 148 which is very reliable and makes a much larger quantity if required. Once made, it must be kept sealed in a plastic bag and used within a month or it will become hard and unusable. It is better to make up the flower paste a few days before you need it so that it is fresh and pliable to work. Flower paste may be coloured or tinted in the usual way with food colourings, or used naturally and coloured with blossom tints or petal dust once it has dried.

Items made with flower paste are not usually edible because of the hardness of the paste. Flower decorations do also use wire, stems, stamens and tape, so it is better just to remove these as keepsakes.

PLUNGER BLOSSOM FLOWERS

These flowers are very useful and versatile: wired or unwired, they may be added to frilled edgings, extension work, used for border work or incorporated into sprays of flowers to give a soft effect.

Flower paste or sugar paste may be used to make these flowers, but if you need to wire them on to stems to make sprays, flower paste is so much stronger and holds its shape better. If you wish to wire sprays together, the flowers need to be set exceptionally hard, otherwise they shatter and break while being wired.

Tint or colour the flower paste to the shade you require. On a lightly cornfloured (cornstarched) surface, roll out the flower paste very thinly so that you can see through the paste. Cut out the flower shape using a large, medium or small plunger blossom cutter and place it on a piece of foam sponge. Eject the flower by pressing the plunger into the sponge to bend the paste into the shape of the flower required. Repeat this process to make a variety of small, medium and large blossoms.

If the flowers are to have a stamen in the centre, make a pin hole in each blossom as it is made. When the blossoms are dry, pipe a bead of royal icing on the back of each stamen and thread it through the sugar blossom to secure. Turn the blossoms upside down to dry. When the blossoms are completely dry, store them in a box between sheets of tissue paper or wire them together using fine florists' wire to make sprays.

TO WIRE THE BLOSSOMS INTO SPRAYS

To make such blossom flowers into sprays, you will need for each a length of about 10 cm (4 in) of 28–30 gauge florists' wire and tape. For a good balance, make up the sprays of three large blossoms, four medium blossoms and five small ones; wire the small blossoms at the end of the spray with the medium and large blossoms mixed in.

Make a hook at the end of the wire and place the stamen through the hook and squeeze together to secure. Attach the tape just next to the back of the blossom and twist it between the fingers to cover about 1 cm (½ in) of the wire and the stamen. Attach another blossom and continue to wrap the tape around the stems to join the blossoms securely together. When you have added the number of blossoms required, continue to wrap the tape around the remaining stem to neaten.

Make as many assorted sprays of blossom flowers as required. Store them in a warm dry place in a box in between layers of tissue paper until they are needed.

To Make Plunger Blossom Sprays

1 Using large, medium and small plunger blossom cutters, cut out several flower shapes in each size and press them on to a piece of foam sponge. Make a pin hole in the centre of each blossom for the stamen and allow the blossoms to dry.

2 Pipe a bead of royal icing on the back of a stamen and thread it through the hole in the blossom to secure. Repeat with the remaining blossoms and leave to dry upside down.

3 Take a 10 cm (4 in) length of florists' wire and make a hook at one end. Place the hook around the stamen at the back of the blossom and squeeze together to secure. Repeat for the remaining blossoms. Take one wired blossom and bind with florists'

tape from the back of the blossom and down to cover about 1 cm (½ in) of the wire and stamen. Add another blossom and continue to wrap the stems with the tape. Continue in this way adding as many blossoms as you require and finish by binding the exposed wires with tape.

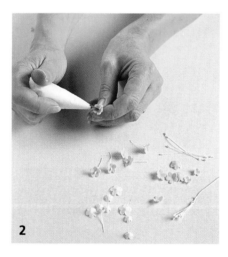

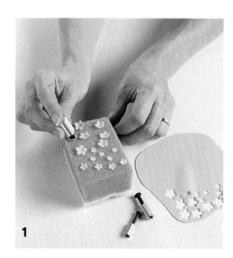

CUT-OUT SUGAR FLOWERS

Cut-out flowers are very simple to make using special cutters available in many different designs. Such cutters are available from all cake-icing and decorating shops. Some of the most popular flower designs include daisy, sweet pea, lily of the valley, Christmas rose, bluebell, carnation, daffodil, fuchsia, foxglove but there are many more to choose from. Leaf cutters and calyx cutters may also be purchased to match the particular flower.

Flower paste and food colouring, 26–28 gauge florists' wire and tape are all needed to make these flowers, but the flowers may also be made without the wire so they may be applied directly to the cake. All these flowers are best made with flower paste so that the petals are paper thin and look very delicate. ▶

TO MAKE A FLOWER CALYX

There are three sizes of calyx cutters, so just match the sizes to the size of the flower you are making. Sometimes small blossom or small star-shaped cutters are more suitable for tiny flowers.

Roll out green flower paste thinly and cut out the shapes. Place the calyx on a flower mat and soften the edges with a dog-bone tool. Thread the calyx on to the back of the flower and secure with a little gum glaze. Alternatively, make the calyx using the Mexican-hat method (see pages 130–131).

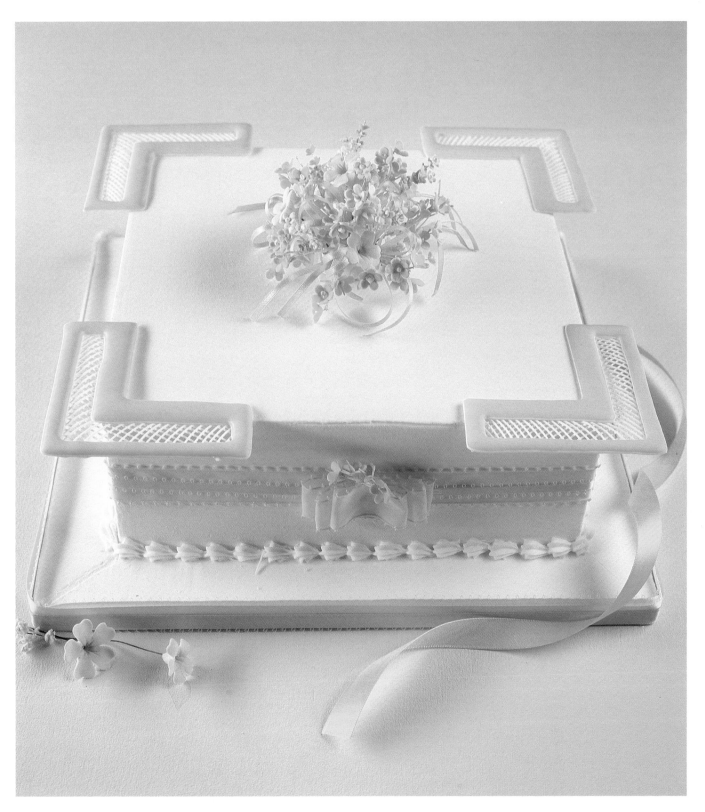

Blossom Spray Cake
A cake for any occasion, just select the colour of your choice. The run-out corner pieces enlaced with trellis work give this royal-iced cake its regal appearance. The centre arrangement is made up of plunger blossom sprays and ribbon loops and a few primroses to give the height. These are all secured in a ball of sugar paste and left to set. The flowers will make a beautiful keepsake.

To Make a Daisy

1 Roll out some white flower paste thinly on a board lightly sprinkled with cornflour (cornstarch) and cut out the shape using a daisy cutter. Ensure the daisy is not sticking to the work surface. Using a cocktail stick (toothpick), frill the petals and place the daisy on a piece of foam. Press the centre to cup the daisy. Take a small pea-sized piece of dark-green paste, make it into a cone shape and roll out the edges thinly. Using a calyx cutter, cut out the shape.

2 Make a hook at the end of a 7.5 cm (3 in) piece of 26 gauge wire. Dip the wire into gum glaze and pull it down through the centre of the calyx. Place a small piece of green paste over the hook. Place the daisy on the prepared calyx, sticking it in place with gum glaze. Press the centre lightly with a modelling tool to secure.

3 To make the flower centre, take a pea-sized piece of dark-yellow flower paste and press it on a sieve to pattern the surface.

Attach the flower centre to the daisy with gum glaze and dust lightly around the base of the petals with moss-green blossom tints.

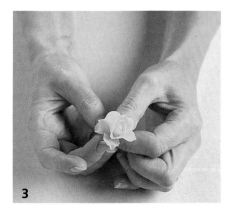

To Make a Rose

1 Make a hook at the end of a piece of 26 gauge wire and dip it in gum glaze. Mould a cone of flower paste around it and leave it to dry. Roll out some paste thinly on a board lightly dusted with cornflour (cornstarch) and cut out three shapes in three sizes using a rose cutter.

2 Using a modelling tool, roll the petals to soften.

3 Thread one petal on the wired cone, secure with gum glaze and then secure the second and third petals so that each is around and over the first.

4 Cut out a green calyx using a rose-shaped calyx cutter and brush with gum glaze. Thread the rose through the calyx and secure in position. Mould a tiny piece of green paste into a cone and thread on to the wire and secure to the calyx. Dust with blossom tints to highlight the rose, if wished.

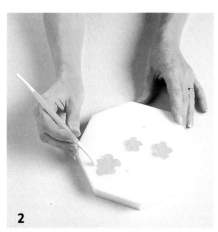

To Make a Sweet Pea

1 Make a hook at the end of a 26 gauge green wire, and dip it into gum glaze. Cover this with a tiny piece of flower paste. Roll out a piece of paste thinly on a board dusted with cornflour (cornstarch) and cut out a petal using the smallest sweet-pea cutter. Brush with a little gum glaze and fold around the centre cone. Press together to form a flat, semi-circular petal shape. Cut out a medium-sized and a large petal. Soften the edges and cup each side of the petals with a modelling tool.

2 Attach the medium-sized petal to the first petal with gum glaze so that it looks like a butterfly.

3 Then attach the largest petal behind the medium-sized one.

4 Cut out a green calyx using a sweet pea calyx cutter. Thread through the cone and attach with gum glaze to the sweet pea. Hook the end and hang upside down to dry.

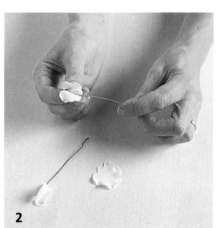

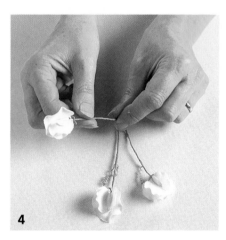

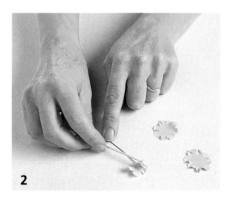

To Make a Carnation

1 Roll a piece of coloured paste out thinly on a board dusted with cornflour (cornstarch). Cut out several flower shapes using a carnation cutter.

Using a modelling knife, make small cuts at intervals around the edges of the petals. Frill the edges using a cocktail stick (toothpick), turning the paste while working and applying lots of pressure to obtain the very fine edges.

2 Make a hook at the end of a piece of 26 gauge wire. Tape the end of the hook with green florists' tape and continue to cover the stem. Carefully place the wire through the centre of one petal. Very lightly brush half the circle with gum glaze and fold up to make a semi-circle. Brush half the petal again with gum glaze and fold over one-third. Turn the petal over and repeat on the other side. Mould the base of the petal very gently on to the wire, hook the end and hang up to dry.

3 Thread two more petals separately on to the wire so that they fall into a natural shape, brushing each with gum glaze. Gently mould the bases and leave to dry upside down.

Good Luck Cake
This horseshoe-shaped rich fruit cake is covered with marzipan and a warm-yellow sugar paste finish. The edges are neatly crimped and the top is decorated with a variety of cut-out sugar flowers, including roses and primroses. This cake would be suitable for a wedding, anniversary, going-away or a new home.

MOULDED OR PULLED FLOWERS

Hand-modelled or pulled flowers are basically those simple flowers made without cutters, and are obviously less complicated than cutter flowers. Small blossom shapes such as forsythia, stephanotis, jasmine, either singly or made into simple sprays, can look very pretty included in a bouquet or arrangement.

The basic equipment required for these flowers is a cone-shaped modelling tool, a modelling knife or scissors, some florists' wire and food colouring or blossom tints. Most of the flowers are made with four, five or six petals.

One simple flower shape is shown below. To make other shaped pulled flowers, copy real blossoms or pictures and follow the same procedure using a cone of paste and flower centre modelling tool to make the shape, then press and pull the petals to match the blossom.

To wire these flowers, make a hook at the end of a piece of 28 gauge wire, dip it into gum glaze and pull through the centre of the flower. Mould the paste to the stem and dry upside down. When dry, dust the flowers with blossom tints, if wished, and wire into sprays.

To Make Pulled Blossom

1 Take a pea-sized piece of paste and make a cone shape. Dust the modelling tool with cornflour (cornstarch) and insert it into the thick end of the cone shape.

2 Either cut against the tool with a modelling knife, or remove and cut with scissors to make five even-sized petals.

3 Open up the flower by gently pressing the petals backwards. Shape one petal at a time, pressing it between the thumb and the finger to flatten the shape. Pinch the end of the petal to round it slightly, then soften and thin the petal by gently pulling with your thumb on top and forefinger underneath. Repeat this action with each petal to complete the flower, keeping the petals and therefore the flower even in size.

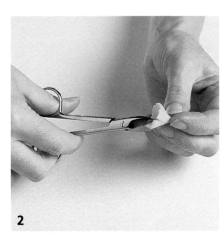

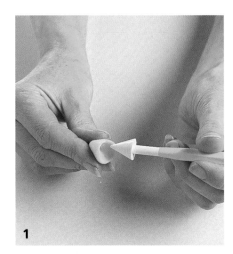

Moulded Rose

1 Make a cone shape of sugar paste or flower paste. Press out each petal individually and wrap around the cone shape, covering it at the top with the first petal. Add a second petal so that the join of the first petal is in the centre of the second petal.

2 Keep adding more petals, gently shaping and curling the edges to give a realistic shape. Work the rose off the cone shape, using your forefingers to roll the stem thinly enough to separate the rose from the cone.

3 When the rose is dry, gently brush the petals with petal dust to give a hint of colour.

MEXICAN-HAT FLOWERS

This method of making flowers is in effect a combination of the pulled blossom and cut-out techniques already described, and can be applied to several flower shapes and can be used for making calyces too. The results are very effective.

To Make a Primrose

1 Mould a piece of pale-yellow flower paste into a cone shape and press out the edges thinly keeping the centre cone thin. Place it upside down on an acrylic board. Using a thin modelling tool, lightly roll all the way around the cone to make the circle very thin with a fine cone shape in the centre.

2 Using a primrose cutter, place it over the cone on to the paste and cut out the shape.

3 Remove the cutter, hold the cone in one hand and press a pointed modelling tool with a ridged side into the centre of the cone to shape the flowers. Soften the petals with a dog-bone modelling tool on a flower mat with the cone end in the hole. Leave upside down on foam to dry.

4 If you are inserting wire or stamens, insert the hooked wire dipped into gum glaze. If the flowers are very delicate, mould a tiny piece of paste around the wire before inserting. Leave upside down to dry, then colour with petal dust.

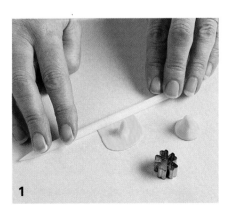

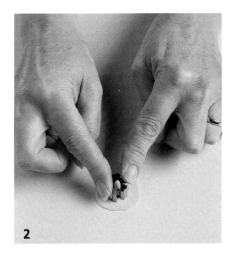

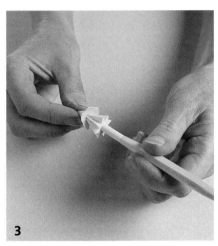

To Make a Fuchsia

1 Take four pink stamens and fold three in half, keeping one longer. Wrap a fine piece of wire around the stamens and attach them securely to a length of 30 gauge wire with green florists' tape.

Roll out a piece of paste very thinly and cut out five petal shapes using a small petal-shaped cutter. Brush the edges of each with gum glaze and arrange them in a line, overlapping each petal slightly.

Shape a piece of flower paste into a cone. Press the wide end flat, keeping a thin cone shape in the centre. Place the cone on an acrylic board and, using a thin modelling tool, roll out the edges until very thin, keeping the cone in the centre thin enough to place the fuchsia cutter over. Cut out the cone shape with the fuchsia cutter and make a cavity in the centre of the cone with the thin modelling tool.

2 Loosely roll up the group of five petals, pressing the pointed ends together to make a petal cone. Thread the stamens through the centre, brushing the neck of the stamens with gum glaze. Press to fit around the wire. Hang upside down to dry for 10 minutes.

Place the fuchsia cone into the hole on the flower mat, and soften and curl the petals using a dog-bone tool. Brush the centre with gum glaze and carefully thread the stamens wire through the centre of the petals to fit firmly.

3 Bend each petal slightly backwards to give a realistic appearance. Hang the flower upside down to dry, and then dust with pink and purple petal dust.

3 Place the shapes on a flower mat, with the cone shape in the hole so the cone does not get damaged while working the petals. Soften the edge and centre of each petal using a dog-bone modelling tool gently to curl, enlarge and cup the petal shape.

4 Take the cone-shaped petal and brush the centre with a little gum glaze. Place the remaining petal on top so the petals fall in between the cone petals. Thread the stamens carefully through the centre, brushing the top stamens with gum glaze and pull through so only the stamens and no wire show inside the freesia.

    Bend the petals carefully and hang the flower upside down to dry. Cut out a tiny star calyx and place over the end of each flower.

5 Mould a tiny piece of paste into an elongated shape to make the closed buds. Repeat to make three more buds, each larger than the one before. Make a hole in the base of each bud, dip four stamens into gum glaze and insert each into the buds. Leave to dry.

    To wire into a spray, use a piece of 30 gauge wire. Start with the tiniest buds and attach together on to the end of the wire with tape. Add the remaining buds, positioning them in a line but a little apart and securing them with tape. Continue adding the flowers to complete the spray and bending the wire to its natural shape.

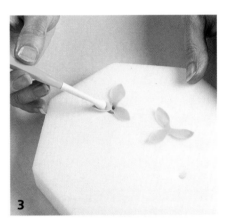

To Make a Freesia Spray

1 Take two stamens, bend them in half and attach them to a piece of 26 gauge green wire. Secure them with florists' tape and cut off the stamen ends.

    To make the freesia flowers, use a small ball of paste shaped into a cone and press the edges very thinly to look like a pixie hat with a point in the centre, which is slim enough for the freesia cutter to cover. Place the cutter over the cone and cut out the shape neatly.

2 Using a thin modelling tool, press it into the centre of the flower to make a hollow cone shape. Roll out a small piece of flower paste thinly and cut out a flat petal shape using the same cutter as before.

LEAVES

There are two methods of making leaves, depending on whether you require ordinary flat cut-out ones or wish to wire leaves to add to sprays of flowers.

To Make Cut-Out and Wired Leaves

1 Colour the flower paste green (vary the shade depending on the type of leaves you are making). For unwired leaves, roll the paste out very thinly and use either leaf cutters or a real leaf to cut around.

For wired leaves, roll the paste out thinly from each side of the centre to form a central ridge. Position the leaf cutter so that the ridge runs down the centre of the leaf and cut out the shape.

2 For both types of leaves, either make vein impressions using real leaves or use a modelling tool to draw veins on the paste.

For unwired leaves, bend the cut-out slightly and dry over dowelling to impart some shape. For wired leaves, dip a 7.5 cm (3 in) length of 28 gauge green wire in gum glaze and insert into the ridge on the back of the leaf. Bend the leaf a little to soften the edges and leave to dry.

3 Finally, brush the leaves with blossom tints to variegate the colour giving a natural effect.

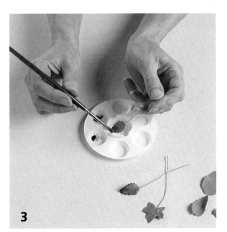

Making a Flower Spray

1 Make a small hook at the end of a length of 28 gauge florists' wire and attach a wired leaf. Secure in position with a piece of green tape by twisting with the fingers. Next, add a blossom spray about 2.5 cm (1 in) down the wire and continue to tape the spray to the wire.

2 Select the size and colour of the wired sugar flowers you need; attach these flowers, one at a time, to the wire and secure them with the tape.

Gently bend the heads of each flower to create a pleasing arrangement; always use tweezers to bend the wire.

3 Finish the spray of flowers, making sure it sits flat on to the surface, and bend the tail into a coil or loop.

Floral Spray Cake
A simple rich fruit cake, covered with marzipan and champagne-coloured sugar paste and trimmed with ribbons – no other decoration is necessary when you make a spray of hand-made sugar flowers.

PASTILLAGE

As flower paste is so strong and dries so hard, it can often be mistaken for fine porcelain. Rolling out the paste thinly and cutting very accurately, the paste can be made into delicate plaques, cards, boxes or moulded items.

All the sugar-craft skills can be combined to make a *pastillage* plaque. Once the shape has been established and cut out, the edges may be frilled, crimped, piped with embroidery or *broderie anglaise* edging.

The plaque can then be designed to include moulded or cut-out flowers, run-outs, appliquéd work or it can be painted by hand. Inscriptions may be written on it, or it may even include modelled figures. Once the plaque is complete, it can sit on a cake as the main decoration; or it may be used as a gift, packaged in a pretty box.

To make a *pastillage* plaque, roll out the flower paste thinly on a lightly dusted surface. Cut out the plaque shape on the surface on which it is to be dried using a sharp knife wielded with a single rocking movement. Do not drag the knife through the paste or it will stretch the paste. Cut in from the corners – not out, as this may cause them to curl up when dry. For small cuts, use round or oval cutters dipped in cornflour (cornstarch), but press down firmly once with the cutter to cut out the shape cleanly. Smooth the edge with the fingers.

Choose the finish required for the edge of the plaque, either leaving it plain or crimping a design around the edge. Using a cocktail stick (toothpick), frill the edge or cut out a *broderie anglaise* design. Allow the plaque to dry in a warm place for at least 12 hours. Once the shape has been cut, it must not be moved until it is dry or it might become distorted.

Plan the design for the plaque: run-outs or motifs may be made and applied; hand-made sugar flowers in sprays may be attached to the plaque and an inscription then piped or written on it with food colouring pens; or moulded items may be applied to make a picture.

Make all the items you require and attach them to the plaque with royal icing. Leave to dry overnight, or place it directly on the iced cake.

To Make a Pastillage *Plaque Decorated With Flowers*

1 Make a 15 cm (6 in) flower paste plaque and crimp the edge.

Mould two full-blown roses and one bud and brush with peach petal dust when dry. Make three daisies, four primroses, two sprays of blossom and four leaves. Make a few ribbon loops to infill the plaque.

2 Secure a piece of sugar paste the size of a walnut in the centre of the plaque. Arrange the flowers and ribbons until you have achieved the right arrangement. Then press all the flowers into the sugar paste, cutting the wires to length, and secure the leaves with a little royal icing.

Brush the plaque lightly with peach blossom tints.

Floral Plaque Cake
*A floral plaque is always a good
stand-by to have for a cake
decoration. It suits almost any
occasion, and, as an added bonus,
may be kept afterwards.*

BASIC RECIPES

No amount of skill in applying icings and decorations will disguise a poorly made cake base or icing – cakes after all are meant to be as delicious as they are attractive to the eye. Armed with these tried-and-tested recipes for classic sponge and fruit cakes and perennially popular icings and frostings, you will have perfect results every time. Handy charts are included so the recipe quantities can be adapted for every size and shape of cake, and there is a wealth of information on calculating quantities, cutting cakes, storing, planning your time and much more.

CAKE-MAKING EQUIPMENT

For successful cake-making you will need a range of items, many of which you may already have in the kitchen. Add to the basics gradually as your skills – and ambitions – progress, and choose good-quality equipment that will last.

EQUIPMENT FOR MAKING CAKES AND ICINGS

Scales: accurate scales for weighing ingredients in metric and imperial are essential for good results.

Measuring jug: an all-purpose one with metric and imperial measurements for liquids in millilitres, fluid ounces or pints.

Standard measuring spoons: these allow spoon measurements which are consistently accurate for both dry and liquid ingredients.

Standard measuring cups: these give a consistently accurate measurement for dry ingredients mainly, and some liquids.

Wooden spoons: a selection of wooden spoons with handles of varying lengths, suitable for beating large or small quantities.

Whisks: a small hand-held rotary whisk and wire whisks are needed for whisking cream or egg whites or light mixtures to obtain volume and give smooth consistencies.

Hand-held electric mixer: this type of mixer is invaluable when making large quantities of cake mixtures (batters) or icings for wedding or other special occasion cakes.

Food processor: ideal for chopping ingredients quickly, beating butter icing or for making cake mixtures.

Spatulas: with a flexible plastic blade, these come in many shapes and sizes and are essential for folding ingre-dients into lightly whipped mixtures or cake batters.

Bowls: get a selection of small, medium and large heatproof bowls in glass or china, with smooth rounded insides which allow thorough even mixing.

Tins (pans) and moulds: always choose the best-quality sturdy tins for baking. Good thickness of metal prevents over-cooking and ensures the tins retain their shape.

Baking sheets: heavy-duty baking sheets which will not warp in the oven are necessary for meringues, pastry or sponge layers. Try to get these without raised edges, but baking sheets which have sides are ideal for standing cake tins on.

Cooling racks: these come in different sizes, either round or oblong in shape and with wide or narrow mesh.

Papers: greaseproof paper, baking parchment, waxed paper and rice

paper all have their own uses: greaseproof paper is best for lining tins; baking parchment is ideal for meringues, spreading melted chocolate and drying moulded or cut-out sugar decorations; waxed paper, being fine and flexible, is ideal for icing run-outs and piped decorations; rice paper is used for meringues.

Glazing brushes: get one small- and one medium-sized brush for brushing tins and moulds with melted fat or oil. Also get one in a larger size for brushing cakes with glaze.

Cutters: a set of plain round and fluted pastry cutters in assorted sizes are always useful. Fancy cookie cutters are available in many sizes.

Palette knives: small, medium and large straight palette knives with flexible blades are necessary for both

loosening cakes from tins and spreading and smoothing icing.

Knives: a selection of small, medium and large knives is useful for preparing ingredients and for cutting cakes into layers.

Ruler, scissors and pencil: are also necessary when making cakes.

Cake boards: are available in many sizes and in different shapes. Use thick cake boards for large iced cakes and wedding cakes, and thin cake boards for light cakes with butter icing or cream.

Boxes: cake boxes are invaluable when making celebration cakes. Once the cakes have been made and placed on a cake board, they can be stored in boxes to keep them clean, dry and free from damage.

Baking Equipment
1. *Baking tins (pans)*
2. *Measuring jug*
3. *Standard measuring spoons*
4. *Standard measuring cups*
5. *Glass heatproof bowls*
6. *Cake box*
7. *Cake boards*
8. *Scissors*
9. *Pencil*
10. *Ruler*
11. *Rice paper*
12. *Baking parchment*
13. *Waxed paper*
14. *Run-out film*
15. *Greaseproof paper*
16. *Cooling rack*
17. *Palette knives*
18. *Sieve*
19. *Sharp knife*
20. *Glazing brush*
21. *Wooden spoon*
22. *Fancy biscuit (cookie) cutters*
23. *Pastry cutters*

CAKES

You may have your own family favourites, but do try these well-tested recipes for classic sponge and fruit cakes – you will be assured of perfect results every time.

RICH FRUIT CAKE

This recipe makes a very moist rich cake suitable for any celebration cake. It allows the cake to be made in stages, especially if time is short or if you are making more than one cake. The fruit may be prepared and soaked overnight and the cake made the following day. Once the mixture (batter) is in the tin (pan), the surface may be covered with greaseproof paper and the cake stored in a cool place overnight (if cooking is not possible on the day). The quantities have been carefully worked out so that the depth of each cake is the same. This is important when making several tiers for a wedding cake as they must all be the same depth.

1 In a large mixing bowl, put the raisins, sultanas (white raisins), currants, glacé cherries, mixed peel, chopped nuts, orange zest and juice, and the brandy or sherry. Mix all the ingredients together until well blended, then cover the bowl with clingfilm (plastic wrap). Leave for several hours or overnight if desired.

2 Preheat the oven to 140°C (275°F/ Gas 1). Grease and line a deep cake tin following the instructions on page 153. See the chart on page 141 for quantities.

3 Sift the flour and mixed spice into another mixing bowl. Add the ground almonds, sugar, butter, treacle (molasses) and eggs. Mix together with a wooden spoon, then beat for 1–2 minutes until smooth and glossy. Alternatively, beat for 1 minute using an electric mixer, especially if large quantities are being made.

4 Gradually add the mixed fruit, folding it into the cake mixture using a spatula, until all the fruit has been evenly incorporated.

5 Spoon the mixture into the prepared tin and spread evenly. Give the tin a few sharp bangs to level the mixture and to remove any air pockets. Smooth the surface with the back of a metal spoon, making a slight depression in the centre. The cake surface may be covered with greaseproof paper and left overnight in a cool place if required.

6 Bake the cake in the centre of the oven, following the chart cooking time. If the mixture has been made and left overnight in a cool place, it will need a slightly longer cooking time. Test the cake to see if it is cooked 15 minutes before the end of the calculated cooking time. The cake should feel firm and when a fine skewer is inserted into the centre, it should come out quite clean. If the cake is not fully cooked, re-test it at 15-minute intervals. Remove the cake from the oven and allow it to cool in the tin.

7 Turn the cake out of the tin, but do not remove the lining paper as it helps to keep the moisture in. When storing cakes add some more alcohol: measure out a similar quantity of alcohol as went into the cake, then spoon half of this over the top of the cooked cake and wrap in double-thickness foil.

Storing Store the cake in a cool dry place on its base with the top uppermost for a week. Unwrap the cake and spoon over the remaining quantity of extra brandy or sherry. Re-wrap well, invert the cake and store it upside down, so the brandy or sherry moistens the top and helps to keep it flat.

The cake will store well for up to 3 months; if it is going to be stored for a longer time, it will be better to freeze it. Make sure it is completely defrosted before marzipanning and icing.

LIGHT FRUIT CAKE

This is a light moist fruit cake, which can be made to replace the rich fruit cake if required. As there is less fruit in the cake, it has a tendency to dome during cooking, so ensure a deep depression is made in the centre of the mixture (batter) before putting it in the oven. It will keep for up to one month once it has been marzipanned and iced.

1 Preheat the oven to 140°C (275°F/ Gas 1). Grease and line a deep cake tin (pan) following the instructions on page 153. See the chart on page 140 for quantities.

2 Place the mixed dried fruit, peel, ginger, glacé cherries, lemon zest, juice and sherry in a large mixing bowl. Mix all these ingredients together until well blended.

3 Sift the flour, mixed spice and sugar into another mixing bowl. Add the butter or margarine and eggs. Mix together with a wooden spoon, then beat for 1–2 minutes until smooth and glossy.

4 Gradually add the mixed fruit and fold it into the cake mixture using a spatula until all the fruit is evenly incorporated. Spoon the mixture into the prepared cake tin and spread it evenly. Give the tin a few sharp bangs to level the mixture and remove any air pockets. Smooth the surface with the back of a metal spoon, making a fairly deep depression in the centre.

5 Bake the cake in the centre of the oven according to the quantity you are making, following the chart cooking time as a guide. Test the cake 15 minutes before the end of the calculated cooking time. If cooked, the cake should feel firm and when a fine skewer is inserted into the centre, it should come out quite clean. If the cake is not fully cooked, re-test at 15-minute intervals. Remove the cake from the oven and leave to cool in the tin.

Storing Wrap in foil and store in a cool place for up to 4 weeks.

LIGHT FRUIT CAKE CHART

| Square cake | 13 cm (5 in) | 15 cm (6 in) | 18 cm (7 in) | 20 cm (8 in) | 23 cm (9 in) | 25 cm (10 in) | 28 cm (11 in) | 30 cm (12 in) |
Round cake	15 cm (6 in)	18 cm (7 in)	20 cm (8 in)	23 cm (9 in)	25 cm (10 in)	28 cm (11 in)	30 cm (12 in)	33 cm (13 in)
Mixed dried fruit	275 g (10 oz/ 1⅔ cups)	400 g (14 oz/ 2⅓ cups)	450 g (1 lb/ 2⅔ cups)	675 g (1 lb 8 oz/ 4 cups)	900 g (2 lb/ 5⅓ cups)	1.1 kg (2 lb 8 oz/ 6⅔ cups)	1.5 kg (3 lb 4 oz/ 8⅔ cups)	1.8 kg (4 lb/ 10⅔ cups)
Cut mixed peel	25 g (1 oz/ ¼ cup)	25 g (1 oz/ ¼ cup)	25 g (1 oz/ ¼ cup)	25 g (1 oz/ ¼ cup)	50 g (2 oz/ ⅓ cup)	75 g (3 oz/ ½ cup)	150 g (5 oz/ 1 cup)	175 g (6 oz/ 1¼ cups)
Stem ginger, chopped	25 g (1 oz/ ¼ cup)	25 g (1 oz/ ¼ cup)	50 g (2 oz/ ⅓ cup)	75 g (3 oz/ ½ cup)	125 g (4 oz/ ¾ cup)	150 g (5 oz/ 1 cup)	200 g (7 oz/ 1⅓ cups)	225 g (8 oz/ 1½ cups)
Glacé cherries, quartered	25 g (1 oz/ ¼ cup)	25 g (1 oz/ ¼ cup)	50 g (2 oz/ ⅓ cup)	75 g (3 oz/ ½ cup)	125 g (4 oz/ ¾ cup)	150 g (5 oz/ 1 cup)	175 g (6 oz/ 1¼ cups)	225 g (8 oz/ 1½ cups)
Lemon zest, grated	1 tsp	1½ tsp	2 tsp	3 tsp	4 tsp	5 tsp	6 tsp	8 tsp
Lemon juice	1 tbsp	1½ tbsp	2 tbsp	2½ tbsp	3 tbsp	3½ tbsp	4½ tbsp	5 tbsp
Sherry	1 tbsp	1½ tbsp	2 tbsp	2½ tbsp	3 tbsp	3½ tbsp	4½ tbsp	5½ tbsp
Plain (all-purpose) flour	225 g (8 oz/ 2 cups)	275 g (10 oz/ 2½ cups)	350 g (12 oz/ 3 cups)	450 g (1 lb/ 4 cups)	575 g (1 lb 4 oz/ 5 cups)	675 g (1 lb 8 oz/ 6 cups)	900 g (2 lb/ 8 cups)	1.1 kg (2 lb 8 oz/ 10 cups)
Ground mixed spice	1 tsp	1½ tsp	2 tsp	3 tsp	4 tsp	5 tsp	6 tsp	8 tsp
Light soft brown sugar	175 g (6 oz/ ¾ cup)	225 g (8 oz/ 1¼ cups)	275 g (10 oz/ 1½ cups)	400 g (14 oz/ 2 cups)	475 g (1 lb 1 oz/ 2⅓ cups)	575 g (1 lb 4 oz/ 2¾ cups)	775 g (1 lb 11 oz/ 3¾ cups)	950 g (2 lb 2 oz/ 4¾ cups)
Butter or margarine, softened	175 g (6 oz/ ¾ cup)	225 g (8 oz/ 1 cup)	275 g (10 oz/ 1¼ cups)	400 g (14 oz/ 1¾ cups)	475 g (1 lb 1 oz/ 2¼ cups)	575 g (1 lb 4 oz/ 2½ cups)	775 g (1 lb 11 oz/ 3⅓ cups)	950 g (2 lb 2 oz/ 4¼ cups)
Eggs (size 3)	3	4	4	5	6	7	9	11
Cooking time	2¼–2½ hrs	2½–2¾ hrs	2¾–3¼ hrs	3¼–3¾ hrs	3½–4 hrs	4–4½ hrs	4½–4¾ hrs	5–5½ hrs

RICH FRUIT CAKE CHART

Square cake Round cake	13 cm (5 in) 15 cm (6 in)	15 cm (6 in) 18 cm (7 in)	18 cm (7 in) 20 cm (8 in)	20 cm (8 in) 23 cm (9 in)	23 cm (9 in) 25 cm (10 in)	25 cm (10 in) 28 cm (11 in)	28 cm (11 in) 30 cm (12 in)	30 cm (12 in) 33 cm (13 in)
Raisins	200 g (7 oz/ 1¼ cups)	250 g (9 oz/ 1½ cups)	300 g (11 oz/ 1¾ cups)	375 g (13 oz/ 2 cups)	425 g (15 oz/ 2½ cups)	575 g (1 lb 4 oz/ 3⅓ cups)	675 g 1 lb 8 oz/ 4 cups)	800 g 1 lb 12 oz/ 4⅔ cups)
Sultanas (white raisins)	125 g (4 oz/ ⅔ cup)	175 g (6 oz/ 1 cup)	225 g (8 oz/ 1⅓ cups)	275 g (10 oz/ 1⅔ cups)	350 g (12 oz/ 2¼ cups)	475 g (1 lb 1 oz/ 3¼ cups)	600 g (1 lb 5 oz/ 3½ cups)	675 g (1 lb 8 oz/ 4 cups)
Currants	75 g (3 oz/ ½ cup)	125 g (4 oz/ ⅔ cup)	175 g (6 oz/ 1 cup)	225 g (8 oz/ 1⅓ cups)	275 g (10 oz/ 1⅔ cups)	400 g (14 oz/ 2⅓ cups)	475 g (1 lb 1 oz/ 2¾ cups)	575 g (1 lb 4 oz/ 4 cups)
Glacé cherries, halved	75 g (3 oz/ ½ cup)	75 g (3 oz/ ½ cup)	150 g (5 oz/ 1 cup)	175 g (6 oz/ 1¼ cups)	200 g (7 oz/ 1⅓ cups)	225 g (8 oz/ 1½ cups)	275 g (10 oz/ 1¾ cups)	350 g (12 oz/ 2¼ cups)
Cut mixed peel	25 g (1 oz/ ¼ cup)	40 g (1½ oz/ ⅓ cup)	50 g (2 oz/ ⅓ cup)	75 g (3 oz/ ½ cup)	125 g (4 oz/ ¾ cup)	175 g (6 oz/ 1¼ cups)	225 g (8 oz/ 1½ cups)	275 g (10 oz/ 1¾ cups)
Chopped mixed nuts	25 g (1 oz/ ¼ cup)	40 g (1½ oz/ ⅓ cup)	50 g (2 oz/ ½ cup)	75 g (3 oz/ ¾ cup)	125 g (4 oz/ 1 cup)	175 g (6 oz/ 1⅔ cup)	225 g (8 oz/ 2¼ cups)	275 g (10 oz/ 2¾ cups)
Orange zest, grated	1 tsp	1½ tsp	2 tsp	2½ tsp	1 tbsp	1½ tbsp	1½ tbsp	2 tbsp
Orange juice	1 tbsp	1½ tbsp	2 tbsp	2½ tbsp	3 tbsp	4 tbsp	5 tbsp	6 tbsp
Brandy or sherry	1 tbsp	2 tbsp	3 tbsp	4 tbsp	5 tbsp	6 tbsp	7 tbsp	8 tbsp
Plain (all-purpose) flour	175 g (6 oz/ 1½ cups)	200 g (7 oz/ 1¾ cups)	250 g (9 oz/ 2¼ cups)	300 g (11 oz/ 2¾ cups)	400 g (14 oz/ 3½ cups)	500 g (1 lb 2 oz/ 4½ cups)	625 g (1 lb 6 oz/ 5½ cups)	725 g (1 lb 10 oz/ 6½ cups)
Ground mixed spice	1 tsp	1½ tsp	2½ tsp	1 tbsp	1¼ tbsp	1½ tbsp	2 tbsp	3½ tbsp
Ground almonds	25 g (1 oz/ ¼ cup)	40 g (1½ oz/ ⅓ cup)	65 g (2½ oz/ ⅔ cup)	125 g (4 oz/ 1 cup)	150 g (5 oz/ 1⅓ cups)	225 g (8 oz/ 2¼ cups)	275 g (10 oz/ 2½ cups)	350 g (12 oz/ 3 cups)
Molasses sugar	125 g (4 oz/ ½ cup)	150 g (5 oz/ ¾ cup)	200 g (7 oz/ 1 cup)	250 g (9 oz/ 1¼ cups)	350 g (12 oz/ 1⅔ cups)	475 g (1 lb 1 oz/ 2⅓ cups)	575 g (1 lb 4 oz/ 2¾ cups)	650 g (1 lb 7 oz/ 3⅓ cups)
Butter, softened	125 g (4 oz/ ½ cup)	150 g (5 oz/ ⅔ cup)	200 g (7 oz/ ¾ cup)	250 g (9 oz/ 1¼ cups)	350 g (12 oz/ 1½ cups)	475 g (1 lb 1 oz/ 2¼ cups)	575 g (1 lb 4 oz/ 2½ cups)	650 g (1 lb 7 oz/ 2¾ cups)
Black treacle (molasses)	½ tbsp	1 tbsp	1½ tbsp	2 tbsp	2½ tbsp	3 tbsp	3½ tbsp	4 tbsp
Eggs (size 3)	2	3	4	5	6	7	8	10
Cooking time	2¼–2½ hrs	2½–2¾ hrs	3–3½ hrs	3¼–3¾ hrs	3¾–4¼ hrs	4–4½ hrs	4½–5¼ hrs	5¼–5¾ hrs

QUICK-MIX CAKE

QUICK-MIX CAKE CHART			
	2 × 18 cm (7 in) round 1 × 20 cm (8 in) round	2 × 20 cm (8 in) round 1 × 23 cm (9 in) round	2 × 23 cm (9 in) round 1 × 25 cm (10 in) round
Self-raising flour	125 g (4 oz/1 cup)	175 g (6 oz/1½ cups)	225 g (8 oz/2 cups)
Baking powder	1 tsp	1½ tsp	2 tsp
Caster (superfine) sugar	125 g (4 oz/½ cup)	175 g (6 oz/¾ cup)	225 g (8 oz/1 cup)
Soft margarine	125 g (4 oz/½ cup)	175 g (6 oz/¾ cup)	225 g (8 oz/1 cup)
Eggs (size 3)	2	3	4
Cooking time	30–40 minutes	40–50 minutes	50–80 minutes

This is a quick versatile recipe for making a traditional sponge cake in different shapes and flavours.

1 Preheat the oven to 170°C (325°F/ Gas 3). Lightly brush the chosen tin (pan) with oil, and line the base and sides with greaseproof paper.

2 Sift the flour and baking powder into a bowl. Add the sugar, margarine and eggs. Mix together with a wooden spoon, then beat for 1–2 minutes until smooth and glossy.

3 Stir in the chosen flavourings, beat until evenly blended and place the mixture (batter) in the prepared tin. Bake in the oven for the time required,

Flavourings (for 2-egg quantity – increase in proportion to suit the quantity being made)

Chocolate: add 1 tbsp cocoa powder blended with 1 tbsp boiling water, or 25 g (1 oz/scant ¼ cup) chocolate dots, melted
Coffee: 2 tsp instant coffee blended with 1 tsp boiling water
Fruit: 2 tsp finely grated orange, lemon or lime zest
Nuts: replace 25 g (1 oz/¼ cup) flour with finely ground nuts

until well risen and pale golden or until the cake springs back when lightly pressed in the centre.

4 Loosen the edges of the cake with a palette knife. Turn out on a wire rack and remove the paper. Invert the cake and leave to cool completely. Decorate and consume within two weeks.

WHISKED SPONGE

WHISKED SPONGE CAKE CHART			
	1 × 20 cm (8 in) round	2 × 20 cm (8 in) round 1 × 23 cm (9 in) round	2 × 23 cm (9 in) round 1 × 25 cm (10 in) round
Eggs	2	3	4
Caster (superfine) sugar	50 g (2 oz/¼ cup)	75 g (3 oz/⅓ cup)	125 g (4 oz/½ cup)
Plain (all-purpose) flour	50 g (2 oz/½ cup)	75 g (3 oz/¾ cup)	125 g (4 oz/1 cup)
Cooking time	20–25 minutes	25–30 minutes	30–50 minutes

1 Preheat the oven to 180°C (350°F/ Gas 4). Lightly brush the chosen tin (pan) with oil and lightly flour. Line the base with greaseproof paper.

2 Whisk together the eggs and sugar in a heatproof bowl until thoroughly blended. Place the bowl over a saucepan of simmering water and whisk the mixture (batter) until thick and pale. Remove the bowl from the saucepan and continue whisking until the mixture is cool and leaves a thick trail on the surface when the beaters are lifted.

3 Sift the flour on to the surface of the mixture and add any flavourings. Using a spatula, carefully fold the flour into the mixture until smooth. Pour the mixture into the prepared tin and bake in the oven for the time

Flavourings (for 2-egg quantity — increase in proportion to suit the quantity being made)	
Chocolate:	replace 15 g (½ oz/1 tbsp) flour with cocoa powder, or add 25 g (1 oz/1 square) plain chocolate, melted
Coffee:	2 tsp instant coffee blended with 1 tsp boiling water
Fruit:	2 tsp finely grated orange, lemon or lime zest
Nuts:	replace 25 g (1 oz/¼ cup) flour with finely ground nuts

required for the size of tin, until well risen and pale golden or until the cake springs back when lightly pressed in the centre.

4 Allow to cool in the tin for 5 minutes, then turn out. Remove the paper, invert and leave to cool completely on a wire rack.

Storing Do not wrap. Place in a tin and store for one week.

GENOESE SPONGE

This is a whisked sponge cake with added butter to give it a firmer texture. It is ideal for cutting into layers for gâteaux, small shapes for iced fancies, or as a base for a celebration cake.

4 eggs (size 3)
125 g (4 oz/½ cup) caster (superfine) sugar
75 g (3 oz/¾ cup) plain (all-purpose) flour
75 g (3 oz/⅓ cup) unsalted butter, melted and cooled slightly

1 Preheat the oven to 180°C (350°F/ Gas 4). Lightly brush a 20 cm (8 in) square or a 23 cm (9 in) round deep cake tin (pan) with oil and line the base and sides with greaseproof paper.

2 Whisk together the eggs and caster sugar together in a heatproof bowl until thoroughly blended. Place the bowl over a saucepan of simmering water and whisk until thick and pale. Remove the bowl from the saucepan and continue whisking until the mixture (batter) is cool and leaves a

Flavourings	
Chocolate:	50 g (2 oz/2 squares) plain (semi-sweet) chocolate, melted
Coffee:	2 tsp instant coffee dissolved in 1 tsp boiling water
Fruit:	2 tsp finely grated orange, lemon or lime zest

thick trail on the surface when the beaters are lifted.

3 Sift the flour over the surface of the mixture and, using a spatula, carefully fold in the flour, butter (taking care to leave any sediment behind) and any flavourings until the mixture is smooth and evenly blended.

4 Place the mixture in the prepared tin and bake in the oven for 40–45 minutes until well risen and pale golden, or until the cake springs back when lightly pressed in the centre.

5 Allow to cool in the tin for 5 minutes, then turn out. Remove the paper, invert and leave to cool completely on a wire rack.

Storing Wrap the cake in foil or clingfilm (plastic wrap) and place in a tin or cake box. Store for up to two weeks.

MADEIRA CAKE

A good plain cake which can be flavoured and made as an alternative to a light or rich fruit cake. It has a firm moist texture, and makes a good base for marzipanning, icing and decorating.

1 Preheat the oven to 170°C (325°F/Gas 3). Grease and line a deep cake tin (pan) following the instructions on page 153. See the chart below for quantities.

2 Sift the flour and baking powder into a mixing bowl, add the sugar, margarine, eggs and lemon juice. Mix together with a wooden spoon, then beat for 1–2 minutes until smooth and glossy. Alternatively, use an electric mixer and beat for 1 minute only or until the mixture is light and glossy. Do not over-mix.

3 Add any flavourings, if using, and mix until well blended.

4 Place the mixture (batter) into the prepared tin and spread evenly. Give

Flavourings (for 3-egg quantity — increase in proportion to suit the quantities being made)

Cherry: 175 g (6 oz/1¼ cups) glacé cherries, halved
Citrus: replace the lemon with orange or lime juice and 1 tsp of grated orange or lime zest
Coconut: 50 g (2 oz/1 cup) desiccated (shredded) coconut
Nuts: replace 125 g (4 oz/1 cup) flour with ground almonds, hazelnuts, walnuts or pecan nuts

the tin a sharp tap to remove any air pockets. Make a depression in the centre of the mixture to ensure a level surface when cooked.

5 Bake the cake in the centre of the oven following the cooking times in the chart or until the cake springs back when lightly pressed.

6 Leave the cake to cool in the tin, then remove and cool completely on a wire rack.

Storing Wrap in clingfilm (plastic wrap) or foil and store in a cool place for up to two weeks.

MADEIRA CAKE CHART

	15 cm (6 in)	18 cm (7 in)	20 cm (8 in)	23 cm (9 in)	25 cm (10 in)	28 cm (11 in)	30 cm (12 in)
Square cake	15 cm (6 in)	18 cm (7 in)	20 cm (8 in)	23 cm (9 in)	25 cm (10 in)	28 cm (11 in)	30 cm (12 in)
Round cake	18 cm (7 in)	20 cm (8 in)	23 cm (9 in)	25 cm (10 in)	28 cm (11 in)	30 cm (12 in)	33 cm (13 in)
Plain (all-purpose) flour	225 g (8 oz/ 2 cups)	350 g (12 oz/ 3 cups)	450 g (1 lb/ 4 cups)	500 g (1 lb 2 oz/ 4½ cups)	575 g (1 lb 4 oz/ 5 cups)	675 g (1 lb 8 oz/ 6 cups)	900 g 2 lb/ 8 cups)
Baking powder	1 tsp	1½ tsp	2 tsp	2½ tsp	3 tsp	3½ tsp	4 tsp
Caster (superfine) sugar	175 g (6 oz/ ¾ cup)	275 g (10 oz/ 1½ cups)	400 g (14 oz/ 1¾ cups)	450 g (1 lb/ 2 cups)	500 g (1 lb 2 oz/ 2¼ cups)	625 g (1 lb 6 oz/ 2¾ cups)	725 g (1 lb 10 oz/ 3¼ cups)
Soft margarine	175 g (6 oz/ ¾ cup)	275 g (10 oz/ 1¼ cups)	400 g (14 oz/ 1¾ cups)	450 g (1 lb/ 2 cups)	500 g (1 lb 2 oz/ 2¼ cups)	625 g (1 lb 6 oz/ 2¾ cups)	725 g (1 lb 10 oz/ 3¼ cups)
Eggs (size 3)	3	5	7	8	10	12	13
Lemon juice	2 tbsp	3 tbsp	3½ tbsp	4 tbsp	4½ tbsp	5 tbsp	5½ tbsp
Cooking time	1¼–1½ hrs	1½–1¾ hrs	1¾–2 hrs	1¾–2 hrs	2–2¼ hrs	2¼–2½ hrs	2½–2¾ hrs

ICINGS & FROSTINGS

Many different types of icings and frostings have been mentioned in the preceding chapters; here are the recipes. They have been tried and tested many times, so if you follow the instructions and quantities carefully you will have the perfect icings for practising your icing and decorating skills.

CHOCOLATE ICING

This is a rich glossy icing which sets like chocolate fudge, yet it is versatile enough to coat smoothly, swirl or pipe. All these different effects can be achieved, depending on the temperature of the icing when it is used.

To coat and fill a 20 cm (8 in) cake

125 g (4 oz/4 squares) plain (semi-sweet) chocolate
50 g (2 oz/¼ cup) unsalted butter
1 egg, beaten
175 g (6 oz/1½ cups) icing (confectioners') sugar, sifted

1 Place the chocolate and butter in a heatproof bowl set over a saucepan of hot water.

2 Stir occasionally with a wooden spoon until melted. Add the egg and beat until smooth. Remove the bowl from the saucepan. Stir in the icing sugar, then beat until smooth and glossy.

3 Pour immediately over the cake for a smooth finish, or leave to cool for a thicker spreading or piping consistency.

BUTTER ICING

This most popular and well-known icing is quickly made, using half the weight of butter to icing sugar. The flavour and colour may be varied by adding different flavourings and colourings.

Flavourings	
Citrus:	replace the milk and vanilla flavouring with orange, lemon or lime juice and 2 tsp finely grated orange, lemon or lime zest (omit the zest if the icing is to be piped)
Chocolate:	1 tbsp cocoa powder blended with 1 tbsp boiling water, cooled
Coffee:	2 tsp instant coffee blended with 1 tsp boiling water, cooled

To coat and fill a 20 cm (8 in) cake

125 g (4 oz/½ cup) unsalted butter, softened
225 g (8 oz/2 cups) icing (confectioners') sugar, sifted
2 tsp milk
1 tsp vanilla flavouring

1 Place the butter in a bowl. Using a wooden spoon or an electric mixer, beat until light and fluffy.

2 Stir in the icing sugar, milk and vanilla flavouring until evenly mixed. Then beat the icing well until light and smooth.

A richly flavoured frosting using brown sugar and treacle, this is useful for quickly coating any sponge cake with a smooth or swirled finish.

To coat and fill a 20 cm (8 in) cake

75 g (3 oz/¹⁄₃ cup) unsalted butter
3 tbsp milk
25 g (1oz/2 tbsp) soft light brown sugar
1 tbsp black treacle (molasses)
350 g (12 oz/3 cups) icing (confectioners') sugar, sifted

1 Place the butter, milk, sugar and treacle in a heatproof bowl over a saucepan of simmering water. Using a wooden spoon, stir occasionally until

QUICK FROSTING

Flavourings

Coffee:	replace the treacle with 1 tbsp instant coffee
Chocolate:	sift 1 tbsp cocoa powder with the icing sugar
Fruit:	replace the treacle with golden syrup and add 2 tsp of finely grated orange, lemon or lime zest

the butter and sugar have melted.

2 Remove the bowl from the saucepan. Stir in the icing sugar, then beat until smooth and glossy.

3 Immediately pour the frosting over the cake for a smooth finish, or first allow to cool for a thicker spreading consistency.

This icing takes a little more time to make, but it is well worth it for the rich, smooth, light texture of the *crème*, which is suitable for spreading, filling or piping special cakes and gâteaux. For the best results, use it as soon as it is made, or keep it at room temperature for a few hours. Do not re-beat or it will curdle.

To coat a 20 cm (8 in) cake

4 tbsp water
75 g (3 oz/¹⁄₃ cup) caster (superfine) sugar
2 egg yolks
150 g (5 oz/²⁄₃ cup) unsalted butter, softened

1 Place the water in a small saucepan and bring to the boil. Remove the saucepan from the heat and stir in the sugar. Heat gently until the sugar has completely dissolved, then remove the spoon.

2 Boil the mixture rapidly until it becomes syrupy, or until thread stage is reached. To test for this, remove the pan from the heat and place a little syrup on the back of a dry teaspoon.

CRÈME AU BEURRE

Flavourings

Citrus:	replace the water with orange, lemon or lime juice and 2 tsp finely grated orange, lemon or lime zest
Chocolate:	50 g (2 oz/2 squares) plain (semi-sweet) chocolate, melted
Coffee:	2 tsp instant coffee, dissolved in 1 tsp boiling water, cooled

Press a second teaspoon on to the syrup and gently pull them apart. The syrup should form a fine thread. If not, return the saucepan to the heat, boil rapidly and re-test at one-minute intervals.

3 Whisk the egg yolks together in a bowl. Continue whisking while slowly adding the sugar syrup in a steady stream. Whisk until the mixture becomes thick, pale and cool, and leaves a trail on the surface when the beaters are lifted.

4 Beat the butter in a separate bowl until light and fluffy. Add the egg mixture gradually to the creamed butter, beating well after each addition until thick and fluffy.

5 Using a spatula, fold in the chosen flavouring until evenly blended.

MARZIPAN

Homemade marzipan always has that special flavour and texture, so it is well worth making.

Makes 450 g (1 lb)

225 g (8 oz/2¼ cups) ground almonds
125 g (4 oz/½ cup) caster (superfine) sugar
125 g (4 oz/1 cup) icing (confectioners') sugar, sieved
1 tsp lemon juice
few drops of almond flavouring
white of 1 (size 2) egg

1 Place the ground almonds and the sugars in a bowl. Stir until evenly mixed.

2 Make a 'well' in the centre and add the lemon juice, almond flavouring and enough egg white to mix to a soft but firm dough, using a wooden spoon.

3 Lightly dust the work surface with sieved icing sugar and knead the marzipan until smooth and free from cracks.

Storing Wrap in clingfilm (plastic wrap) or store in a plastic bag until ready for use.
  Use the homemade marzipan for covering cakes before applying sugar paste or royal icing (see pages 32–34 for detailed instructions). Alternatively, use to make moulded or

modelled decorations; tint with food colouring, if required (see page 48).

SUGAR PASTE

Although sugar paste is more convenient to buy ready-made, it is useful to have a recipe just in case you run out.

Makes about 575 g (1 lb 4 oz)

1 egg white
2 tbsp liquid glucose
2 tsp rose water
450 g (1 lb/4 cups) icing (confectioners') sugar, sieved, plus more to dust

1 Place the egg white, liquid glucose and rose water in a clean bowl and mix together to break up the egg white. Add the icing sugar and mix together with a wooden spoon until

the icing begins to bind together. Knead together with the fingers until the mixture forms into a ball. Place on a surface lightly dusted with icing sugar and knead until smooth and free from cracks.

2 If the icing is too soft to handle and is sticky, knead in some more sieved icing sugar until firm and pliable. Also if the sugar paste dries out and becomes hard, knead in a little boiled and cooled water until the icing is soft and pliable.

Storing Wrap the sugar paste well in clingfilm (plastic wrap) or store in a plastic bag, making sure that all the air inside the bag has been excluded.

SUGAR PASTE AND MARZIPAN QUANTITIES

Square cake	13 cm (5 in)	15 cm (6 in)	18 cm (7 in)	20 cm (8 in)	23 cm (9 in)	25 cm (10 in)	28 cm (11 in)	30 cm (12 in)
Round cake	15 cm (6 in)	18 cm (7 in)	20 cm (8 in)	23 cm (9 in)	25 cm (10 in)	28 cm (11 in)	30 cm (12 in)	33 cm (13 in)
Sugar paste/ Marzipan	450 g (1 lb)	675 g 1 lb 8 oz)	800 g (1 lb 12 oz)	900 g (2 lb)	1.1 kg (2 lb 8 oz)	1.4 kg (3 lb)	1.6 kg (3 lb 8 oz)	1.8 kg (4 lb)

FLOWER PASTE

Flower paste is used only for making cake decorations. It is exceptionally strong and can be moulded into very fine flowers or cut into individual sugar pieces which dry very quickly. It can also be purchased commercially in a ready-to-mix powdered form, or ready-made, known as 'petal paste' which is very convenient for small quantities but is rather expensive for large quantities. The ingredients – liquid glucose and gum tragacanth – are available from chemists (drug stores) or cake-icing specialists.

Makes 225 g (1/2 lb)

225 g (8 oz/2 cups) icing (confectioners) sugar, sieved
1 tbsp gum tragacanth, sieved
1 rounded tsp liquid glucose
1–2 tbsp cold water

1 Sift the icing sugar and gum tragacanth into a bowl. Make a 'well' in the centre and add the liquid glucose and 1 tbsp water. Mix together with the fingers to form a soft paste and knead on a surface dusted well with icing sugar until smooth, white and free from cracks.

Storing and using Place in a plastic bag or wrap in clingfilm (plastic wrap) and seal well to exclude all the air. Leave the flower paste for two hours before use. Then re-knead and use small pieces at a time, leaving the remaining flower paste well sealed. Use a little white vegetable fat instead of icing sugar when kneading, rolling out or moulding to prevent the paste from becoming dry, and to make it more pliable and easier to handle. It will keep for up to one month.

GUM GLAZE

This is much better than egg white for sticking flower petals together, or sugar paste items. It dries quickly and sets the flower paste.

1 tbsp gum arabic
3 tbsp warm water

Blend the gum arabic with the water until smooth and free from lumps. Place in a tiny screw top jar or container and use as needed.

ROYAL ICING (USING EGG ALBUMEN)

Dried powdered egg white is known as egg albumen and may be used in place of fresh egg whites for royal icing. Simply blend the egg albumen with water to reconstitute it as directed on the packet, then just add the icing (confectioners') sugar. It is more convenient to use as there are no excess egg yolks and it produces a good light glossy icing which is easy to handle for all types of icing. Used as flat icing for tiered cakes, it sets hard enough to support the weight of the cakes, but still cuts easily without being brittle.

Makes 450 g (1 lb/3 1/2 cups)

1 tbsp dried egg albumen, sieved
6 tbsp tepid water
450 g (1 lb/4 cups) icing (confectioners') sugar, sieved

1 Sieve the egg albumen into a clean bowl. Using a clean wooden spoon, gradually stir in the water and blend well together until the liquid is smooth and free from lumps.

2 Mix in enough icing sugar to give the mixture the consistency of unwhipped cream. Continue mixing and adding small quantities of icing sugar every few minutes until the desired consistency has been reached, mixing well and gently beating after each addition. The icing should be smooth glossy and light – almost like a cold meringue in texture, but not aerated. Do not add too much icing sugar too quickly, as this will produce a dull heavy icing.

3 Allow the icing to settle before using it. Cover the surface with a piece of damp clingfilm (plastic wrap) and seal well, excluding all the air.

4 Stir the icing thoroughly before use as this will disperse the air bubbles. Then adjust the consistency, if necessary, by adding more sieved icing sugar or reconstituted egg albumen. Alternatively, for large quantities of royal icing, use a food mixer on the lowest speed.

5 This icing is suitable for flat or peaked icing, piping and run-outs.

Note: use double-strength dried egg albumen for run-outs so that the run-out pieces set hard enough to remove from the paper.

ROYAL ICING (USING FRESH EGG WHITES)

This icing is traditionally used to cover celebration cakes. According to the consistency made, it may be used for flat icing, peaked icing, run-outs or piping designs on cakes.

Makes 450 g (1 lb/3 1/2 cups)

whites of 2 (size 3) eggs
1/4 tsp lemon juice
450 g (1 lb/4 cups) icing (confectioners') sugar, sieved
1 tsp glycerine

1 Place the egg white and lemon juice in a clean bowl. Using a clean wooden spoon, stir thoroughly to break up the egg whites.

2 Mix in enough icing sugar to give the mixture the consistency of unwhipped cream. Continue mixing and adding small quantities of icing sugar every few minutes until the desired consistency has been reached, mixing well and gently beating after each addition. The icing should be smooth glossy and light, almost like a cold meringue in texture but not aerated. Do not add the icing sugar too quickly or it will produce a dull heavy icing which will be difficult to handle. Stir in the glycerine until the icing is well blended.

3 Allow the icing to settle before using it. Cover the surface with a piece of damp clingfilm (plastic wrap) and seal well, excluding all the air.

4 Stir the icing thoroughly before use as this will disperse the air bubbles. Then adjust the consistency, if necessary, by adding more sieved icing sugar. Alternatively, for large quantities of royal icing, use a food mixer on the lowest speed.

5 This icing is suitable for flat or peaked icing, piping and run-outs.

Note: omit the glycerine when making run-outs.

Royal-icing quantity guide It is always difficult to estimate how much royal icing will be needed to ice a cake. The quantity varies considerably according to how the icing is applied, how thick the layers and the number of layers. The design also has to be taken into consideration, whether it is just a piping design or a number of run-outs and sugar pieces.

The best guide to follow when icing cakes is to make up the royal icing in small batches using 900 g (2 lb) of icing sugar, which is double the quantity of the recipes on the opposite page. Each batch of icing made is fresh and free from any impurities which may occur when larger quantities of royal icing are made for one cake. This way you can assess how much more icing you require to finish a cake.

The chart (right) is a guide for covering each cake with two or three thin layers of flat royal icing.

QUANTITY OF ROYAL ICING	CAKE SIZE
450 g (1 lb)	13 cm (5 in) square 15 cm (6 in) round
675 g (1 lb 8 oz)	15 cm (6 in) square 18 cm (7 in) round
900 g (2 lb)	18 cm (7 in) square 20 cm (8 in) round
1.1 kg (2 lb 8 oz)	20 cm (8 in) square 23 cm (9 in) round
1.4 kg (3 lb)	23 cm (9 in) square 25 cm (10 in) round
1.6 kg (3 lb 8 oz)	25 cm (10 in) square 28 cm (11 in) round
1.8 kg (4 lb)	28 cm (11 in) square 30 cm (12 in) round
2 kg (4 lb 8 oz)	30 cm (12 in) square 33 cm (13 in) round

APRICOT GLAZE

It is always a good idea to make a large quantity of apricot glaze, especially when making celebration cakes. Use for brushing the cakes before applying the marzipan, or for glazing fruits on gâteaux and cakes.

Makes 450 g (1 lb/3¹/₂ cups)

*450 g (1 lb/3¹/₂ cups) apricot
jam (jelly)
3 tbsp water*

1 Place the jam and water in a saucepan and heat gently, stirring occasionally until melted.

2 Boil rapidly for 1 minute, then strain through a sieve. Using a wooden spoon, rub through as much of the fruit as possible, discarding the skins left in the sieve.

Storing Pour the glaze into a clean hot jar. Seal with a clean lid and leave to cool. It can be refrigerated for up to 2 months.

GLACÉ ICING

This is an instant icing used for quickly coating and finishing the tops of large or small cakes. By introducing another colour icing, it is also used to make feathered icing.

***To coat the top of a 20 cm (8 in)
cake***

*225 g (8 oz/2 cups) icing
(confectioners') sugar
2–3 tbsp hot water*

1 Sift the icing sugar into a bowl. Using a wooden spoon, gradually stir in enough water to make a mixture the consistency of thick cream.

2 Beat the mixture until white and smooth, and the icing thickly coats the back of a wooden spoon. Colour with a few drops of food colouring, if desired.

3 Use immediately, to cover the top of small or large cakes.

Flavourings

Replace the water with a strong solution of instant coffee, or with freshly squeezed orange, lemon or lime juice.
Sift 2 tsp cocoa powder with the icing sugar for chocolate icing.

CARAMEL

Caramel is the golden brown syrup produced by boiling sugar syrup to an extremely high temperature. It has endless uses both for dipping fruits and nuts, and for drizzling into shapes for decorating. When set, it may also be crushed and used for coating the sides of cakes, or broken into pieces and used as decorations. See pages 62–64 for some decorating ideas.

***Makes enough to coat the sides of
one 20 cm (8 in) cake***

*150 ml (¹/₄ pt/²/₃ cup) water
175 g (6 oz/²/₃ cup) caster (superfine)
sugar*

1 Place the water in a saucepan and bring to the boil. Remove the saucepan from the heat and stir in the sugar. Heat gently until the sugar has completely dissolved, then remove the spoon.

2 Bring to the boil and boil rapidly for several minutes until the bubbles begin to subside and the syrup begins to turn a pale golden brown. Watch carefully at this stage, as the syrup continues to darken when it is taken off the heat.

3 When the caramel is a rich golden brown, it has reached the ideal state for use. Allow the bubbles to subside, then use as required.

STORAGE OF FRUIT CAKES

When cakes are first baked, it is better to leave the lining paper intact when turning the cake out of the tin, as this sealed surface will keep the cake fresh and moist. Wrap the cake in several layers of greaseproof or waxed paper and a final layer of foil. Place the cake on the cake board, with the base uppermost to keep the top flat, and store in a cardboard cake box in a cool dry place for up to one month before applying the marzipan and icing. Do not seal the cake in a tin or plastic container as this may encourage mould growth. The addition of alcohol to a cake mixture (batter) or the baked cake acts as a preservative as well as adding flavour and moisture to the cake. For longer-term storage, it is better to freeze the cake, keeping the flavour in peak condition until it is required.

Lighter fruit cakes or Madeira-type cakes do not keep so well; they are better consumed within one month. So bake, then marzipan, ice and decorate such cakes as soon after they have been made as possible.

When the cake has been marzipanned and iced, it must be stored in a covered cardboard cake box in a warm, dry place. This ensures the icing is kept dry and at peak condition without discolouring or becoming damaged. Damp and cold are the worst conditions for decorated cakes as the icing becomes covered in condensation, discolouring it and causing colours to run.

CALCULATING QUANTITIES AND CUTTING CAKES

Working out the number of servings possible from a round or square cake is extremely simple. Of course, it depends if you intend to serve just a small finger of cake, or a more substantial slice. Whether the cake is round or square, cut across the cake from edge to edge into slices, not wedges, about 2.5 cm (1 in) thick, or thinner if desired. Then cut each slice into 4 cm (1½ in) pieces, or to the size

CAKE PORTION GUIDE

Cake sizes	Round cake portions	Square cake portions
13 cm (5 in)	16	20
15 cm (6 in)	25	30
18 cm (7 in)	36	42
20 cm (8 in)	45	56
23 cm (9 in)	64	72
25 cm (10 in)	81	90
28 cm (11 in)	100	120
30 cm (12 in)	120	140

you require. Allowing for these measurements, it is easy to calculate the number of cake slices you can cut from any given size of cake. On a round cake the slices become smaller at the curved edges, and the first and last slices of the cake are mainly marzipan and icing, so keep this in mind when calculating the servings.

For example: A 20 cm (8 in) square cake will yield about 56 slices according to the measurements above, and a 20 cm (8 in) round cake will yield about 45 slices.

TIME-SCALE FOR CAKE MAKING

This aspect of cake making can often be quite a worry, wondering how much time to allow for making a celebration cake. I find the best way is to work backwards from the date the cake is required.

Firstly, always aim to finish a cake a week before it is required, just in case the person needs the cake earlier or the collection or delivery cannot be made on the day.

Depending on the design of the cake, calculate how long it will take you to decorate one or more cakes. Take into consideration how long the decorations will take you, for example. Add an extra week for intricate run-out collars to allow for drying time, and the same amount of time if you are making hundreds of sugar flowers or sprays.

Sugar paste is much quicker than royal icing so work out the time it will

take to complete either of these icings. To give a rough estimate, allow yourself one week to make a simple cake covered with sugar paste, or ten days to complete a cake with royal icing – both with simple designs. Then allow one or two days for marzipanning, and two days for making the cake.

Take into consideration that decorations can be made in advance and stored carefully so the actual cake will not take as long. If the time-scale appears daunting, remember that you won't actually be working on the cake non-stop; cakes are completed at intervals over a period of time.

HYGIENE AND CLEANLINESS

Celebration cakes are made for special occasions to which many guests will probably be invited – all eager to taste the cake. Therefore it is of the utmost importance that certain rules be observed about hygiene, cleanliness and the use of non-edible cake materials where there is a chance of it affecting somebody's health.

Cakes must always be made in a spotlessly clean environment. All utensils must be clean and well cared for; ingredients must be freshly purchased; tins (pans) carefully lined and prepared; hands scrubbed clean, including fingernails. If you have any sort of cut or abrasion on your hands, cover the area with a coloured plaster so that it may be more easily detected if it comes off.

After the cakes have been cooked, make sure they are wrapped well and stored in a clean, dry place to prevent mould growth. Always use boiled and sieved apricot jam before applying the marzipan to prevent any fermentation between the cake and the marzipan. Once covered, store the cake on a new clean cake board – used ones will harbour bacteria, especially in the scores made when the previous cake was cut. From then on, keep the cake in a new cardboard cake box in a dry place at all times.

Extra care must be taken when covering cakes with royal icing or sugar paste. Otherwise, any small particles of dirt or cake crumbs will get into the icing and they will always come to the surface.

Wear a white overall or cotton shirt so that wool or fabric particles will not get into the icing or on to the work surface where you will be rolling out sugar paste.

Always use white tea towels and white muslin (cheesecloth) so that coloured specks will not get into the icing or on to the cake.

Apply all food colourings with a clean cocktail stick (toothpick) and throw it away afterwards to prevent any contamination or colour mixing. Check very carefully that all the colours used are edible; if you choose to use gold or silver or inedible colours, these pieces of decoration must be labelled as inedible.

Sugar flowers are usually wired with florists' wire, tape, stamens and sometimes coloured with gold and silver colourings. These types of decoration are definitely not edible, and this must be made perfectly clear to the person receiving the cake. Always make wired flowers away from finished cakes, keeping all inedible materials separate.

There are many flowers and decorations which may be made from sugar paste and food tints without the use of wires and stamens, so it should be made clear before starting whether it needs to be all edible or not.

All *pastillage* and wired flower arrangements are made separately and added to the cake last, so ensure these decorations are removed before cutting the cake. The joy of these decorations is that they may be kept as a keepsake, whereas moulded decorations are often eaten.

Silk flowers or fresh flowers look very pretty on cakes as a last-minute decoration. Ensure that the silk flowers are arranged and secured together so they may be removed from the cake easily. Also choose fresh flowers and leaves which are non-poisonous; equally, if they are being sugar-frosted, make sure the flowers are the edible variety.

Gold and silver colours or gold leaf are often used on formal cakes as the appearance looks stunning, but it is not advisable for these decorations to be consumed even though many of them are labelled non-toxic.

The use of ribbons enhances cakes, cake boards and is also used for ribbon insertion. If pins are used to secure ribbons to cakes and cake boards, use stainless-steel pins with bead heads so they may be easily detected, and ensure the recipient knows that pins have been used.

Once any cake has been completed, keep it in the cardboard cake box free from dust and impurities until it is required.

HELP LINE

- For all cake making, ensure you have the correct ingredients for the recipe. Measure every ingredient accurately using standard measuring spoons and jugs and accurate weighing scales.
- Measure the tin (pan) correctly across the base for the right size; tin sizes must match cake quantities, and be prepared according to the recipe.
- Cooking times for cakes are always a guide; always test cake mixtures (batters) a little before the given time. Continue to cook cakes longer if they are not cooked, and test at regular intervals.
- If a quick cake mixture is being cooked in a deep tin such as a loaf tin (bread pan) or pudding basin for a novelty cake, omit the baking powder to ensure the mixture is more stable.
- When marbling sugar paste, knead the leftover trimmings together to form one colour and use it to cover the cake board.
- Mix remaining blossom tints together and keep separately; this is ideal for blending darker colours.
- When using glacé icing to cover a cake or small cakes, cover them in a very thin layer of marzipan before coating.
- Leave glacé icing to stand for a few minutes before using to assess consistency.
- When royal icing a cake smoothly, finish the top or the sides of the cake last according to the design. If the side of the cake is being seen and the top edge is piped, finish the sides last so that the top edge has the finish mark, or vice versa.
- Each time a coat of royal icing is applied to the top of a cake or the side of a round cake, make sure the finish point is different each time. This ensures the cake is level on the top and does not slope, the sides are even and the cake is round.
- Before applying frills on to the sides of a cake or piping extension work which comes near the cake board, pipe the edging design or fit the ribbon first to prevent breakages.
- Piping extension work is very exacting. Pipe the lines of icing on different parts of the design instead of continuing all around the cake. If a thread breaks, it will take the wet threads of icing with it; if they have dried, only one thread will go.

ASSEMBLING CAKES

Cakes iced with royal icing are really quite easy to assemble as the cake pillars are placed directly on the cake and positioned accordingly before placing the next cake on top. If the position is wrong, the cake may be lifted up and the pillars moved.

Aesthetically a cake looks better if the pillars are just underneath the corners of the cake with the cake board proud of the pillars. If they are too close to the centre, the cake looks unbalanced.

Cut out a paper template 5 cm (2 in) smaller than the top of each cake. Fold the template into four and place the pillar on the open corner of the template. Draw around the shape and cut out neatly. Open out the template, place it on the centre of the cake and position the four pillars on the cut spaces of the template. Remove the template and carefully position the next tier.

On a round cake, it looks more balanced to have only three pillars which look like columns. Using a round template, mark it into thirds to position the three pillars.

To assemble sugar paste cakes, acrylic skewers must be inserted into the cakes as the icing will not support the weight. Arrange the cake pillars, which are hollow, on the cake until the position is right, or use the template technique. Insert the skewers right through the icing into the cake until they are resting on the cake board. Mark the skewers level with the top of the pillars, carefully remove the pillars and skewers, and cut the skewers to the correct height. Replace the skewers and the pillars and position the cake.

CAKE SIZES AND CAKE BOARDS

The balance of a tiered wedding cake is most important as the sizes of the tiers can look right or wrong. If the graduation of the sizes of the cake tiers is too steep, the cake looks rather solid and heavy. Likewise, if the gap between the sizes of the tiers is too great, the cake also looks wrong. A good guide to cake-tier spacing is to allow 5–7.5 cm (2–3 in) between each tier. The following sizes give a balanced appearance for a three-tiered cake.

13 + 18 + 23 cm (5 + 7 + 9 in)
15 + 20 + 25 cm (6 + 8 + 10 in)
15 + 23 + 30 cm (6 + 9 + 12 in)

If the cake is only going to have two tiers, the distance between the tiers needs to be slightly greater to give a better balance; about 7.5 cm (3 in).

The cake boards need to be 5–7.5 cm (2–3 in) larger than the cake to allow for the marzipan, icing and decoration. Sometimes this difference is graduated to give a better balance: 5 cm (2 in) on the top tier, 7.5 cm (3 in) on the second tier, and 10 cm (4 in) on the base tier, for example. If the design is protruding over the edge of the cake, such as run-out collars or extension work, allow extra width on the cake boards to prevent damage to the decorations.

LINING A DEEP CAKE TIN (PAN)

For rich fruit cakes, use good-quality fixed-base deep cake tins. Ensure you have the right size of tin for the quantity of cake mixture (batter) – see chart – as this will affect both the depth and the cooking time of the cake. Always measure the tin across the base, not the top.

First, double-line the inside of the tin with greaseproof paper or baking parchment, and then the outside with double-thickness brown paper. This prevents the outside of the cake being over-cooked. Lastly, always stand the tin on a baking sheet lined with three or four thicknesses of brown paper to prevent the base overcooking.

1 Place the tin on double-thickness greaseproof paper or baking parchment and draw around the base. Cut out the marked shape with a pair of scissors.

2 Cut a strip of double-thickness greaseproof paper or baking parchment long enough to wrap around the outside of the tin with a small overlap and to stand 2.5 cm (1 in) above the top of the tin.

3 Brush the base and sides of the tin with melted white fat or oil. Place the cut-out shape in the base of the tin and press flat. Place the double strip of paper inside the tin, pressing well against the sides and making sharp creases where it fits into corners.

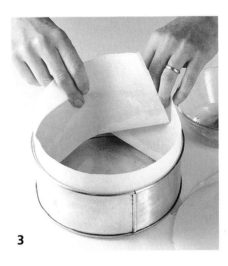

3

4 Brush the base and side paper well with melted white fat or oil. Place a double-thickness strip of brown paper around the outside of the tin and tie securely in place with string.

5 Line a baking sheet with three or four layers of brown paper and stand the tin on top.

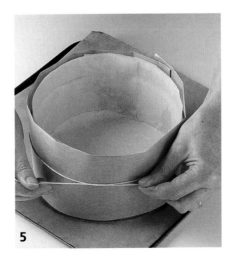

5

TEMPLATES

Several of the templates that appear on the next pages have been used to create some of the cake designs featured in the book and others are shown purely for inspiration. Copy and adapt the designs for your own cakes, but do look out for other sources of inspiration in magazines, greetings cards, embroidery patterns wallpaper books etc, too, for your own individual creations.

If you want to use the templates at the size they appear in the book, simply trace the design on to tracing paper. However, as cakes vary in size you may need to enlarge or reduce the image. The simplest way to do this is by using a photocopier with an en- larging and reducing mode. Alterna- tively, use the grid method. Draw a grid of squares over the chosen tem- plate, then draw another grid on a separate piece of tracing paper to the dimensions you require using the same number of grid lines. Then copy the original design, square by square, on to your new grid.

Alphabets

ABCDEFGHIJ
KLMNOPQRS
TUVWXYZ

ABCDEFGHIJKLMN
OPQRSTUVWXYZ

Run-out corner piece

Broderie anglaise plaque

Run-out motif

Run-out collar template (one-quarter of the design is shown here)

Cut-out appliqué design

INDEX

SUPPLIERS AND USEFUL ADDRESSES

The British Sugarcraft Guild
Wellington House, Messeter Place,
Eltham, London SE9 5DP.

Cake Art Ltd
Wholesale suppliers of icings and
equipment. Unit 16, Crown Close, Crown
Industrial Estate, Priors Wood, Taunton,
Somerset TA2 8RX.

Precision Machine Engineers Ltd
Suppliers of decorating equipment.
Brember Road, South Harrow, Middlesex
HA2 8UN.

Cake Fayre
Suppliers of cake-icing and decorating
equipment. 11 Saddlers Walk, 44 East
Street, Chichester, W Sussex PO19 1HQ.

JF Renshaw Ltd
Suppliers of icings. Mitcham House, River
Court, Albert Drive, Woking, Surrey
GU21 5RP.

Essex Icing Centre
20 Western Road, Billericay, Essex CM12
9DZ.

Invicta Bakeware Ltd
Manufacturers and suppliers of bakery
equipment. Westgate Business Park,
Westgate Carr Road, Pickering, North
Yorkshire YO18 8LX.

Craigmillar
Suppliers of icings and cake mixes.
Stadium Road, Bromborough, Wirral,
Merseyside L62 3NU.

Squires Kitchen
Squire House, 3 Waverley Lane,
Farnham, Surrey GU9 8BB.

Cynthia Venn
3 Anker Lane, Stubbington, Fareham,
Hampshire PO14 3HF.

Rainbow Ribbons
Unit D5, Seedbed Centre, Davidson Way,
Romford, Essex RM7 0AZ.

E Russum & Sons
Edward House, Tenter Street, Rotherham,
South Yorkshire S60 1LB.

The House of Sugarcraft
Suppliers of flower cutters, powder and
paste colours and piping tubes. Unit 10,
Broxhead Industrial Estate, Lindford
Road, Bordon, Hampshire GU35 0NY.

Cel Cakes
Springfield House, Gate Helmsley, York,
North Yorkshire YO4 1NF.

Promodem Ltd
Technical consultancy and suppliers of
QRS and cake tilters. 141 Grange Road,
Great Burstead, Billericay, Essex CM11
2SA.

NORTH AMERICA

**ICES (International Cake Exploration
Society)**
membership enquiries: 3087–30th St.
S.W., Ste.101, Grandville, MI 49418.

Maid of Scandinavia
Equipment, supplies, courses, magazine
Mailbox News. 3244 Raleigh Avenue,
Minneapolis, MN 55416.

Wilton Enterprises Inc
2240 West 75th Street, Woodridge,
Illinois 60517.

Home Cake Artistry Inc
1002 North Central, Suite 511,
Richardson, Texas 75080.

Lorraine's Inc
148 Broadway, Hanover, MA 02339.

Creative Tools Ltd
3 Tannery Court, Richmond Hill, Ontario,
Canada L4C 7V5.

McCall's School of Cake Decorating Inc
3810 Bloor Street, Islington, Ontario,
Canada M9B 6C2.

AUSTRALIA

**Australian National Cake Decorators'
Association**
PO Box 321, Plympton, SA 5038.

Cake Decorating Association of Victoria
President, Shirley Vaas, 4 Northcote
Road, Ocean Grove, Victoria 3226.

**Cake Decorating Guild of New South
Wales**
President, Fay Gardiner, 4 Horsley Cres,
Melba, Act, 2615.

**Cake Decorating Association of
Tasmania**
Secretary, Jenny Davis, 29 Honolulu
Street, Midway Point, Tasmania 7171.

**Cake Decorators' Association of South
Australia**
Secretary, Lorraine Joliffe, Pindari, 12
Sussex Crescent, Morphet Vale, SA 5162.

Fer Lewis, Cake Ornament Company
156 Alfred Street, Fortitude Valley,
Brisbane 4006.

NEW ZEALAND

New Zealand Cake Decorators' Guild
Secretary, Julie Tibble, 78 Kirk Street,
Otaki, Wellington.

Decor Cakes
RSA Arcade, 435 Great South Road,
Otahuhu.

SOUTH AFRICA

South African Sugarcraft Guild
National Office, 1 Tuzla Mews, 187 Smit
Street, Fairlan 2195.

Jem Cutters
PO Box 115, Kloof, 3 Nisbett Road,
Pinetown 3600.